Christiane Wagner

Urban Aesthetics

Christiane Wagner

Urban Aesthetics

Philosophical and social aspects of metropolitan beauty and its reverse side

ScienciaScripts

Imprint

Cover image: www.ingimage.com

This book is a translation from the original published under ISBN 978-3-330-75818-6.

Publisher:
Sciencia Scripts
is a trademark of
Dodo Books Indian Ocean Ltd. and OmniScriptum S.R.L publishing group

120 High Road, East Finchley, London, N2 9ED, United Kingdom
Str. Armeneasca 28/1, office 1, Chisinau MD-2012, Republic of Moldova, Europe
Printed at: see last page
ISBN: 978-620-8-29574-5

index

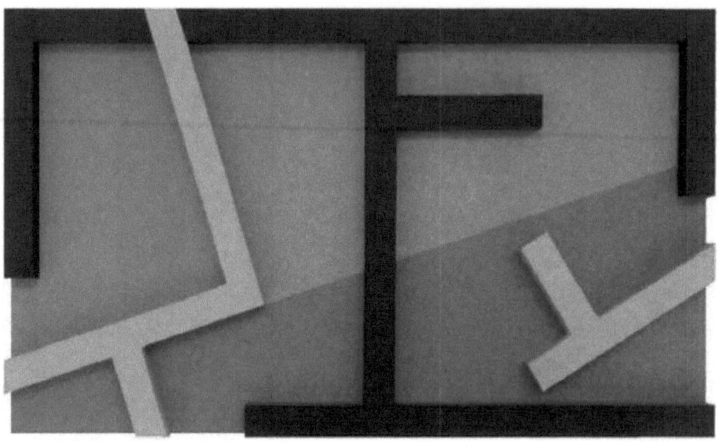

Claudio Tozzi, *Territory*, 2010

Introduction

New forms and contents emerge as processes of transformation that imply values of order and the rules of each culture in the construction of the collective imagination and in the perception of the individual. The contemporary image is formed by the new principles of digital technology, simulating scenarios and environments through a sense of innovation in the configuration of urban spaces. However, the study of the image is directed towards different conceptions and new forms in the context of creation and aesthetics prevalent today, in order to understand the process of new paradigms. Of equal importance is the result of technical procedures in visual programming as solutions to the risk of illusion in the communication and signage systems of large cities. As such, it is interesting to know what would designate and condition the arts to change - in contrast to their observers' own definitions - through innovation in the contemporary image.

Forms and content in the urban space are such common subjects explored by the *media* from time to time on contemporary art, in France, Sao Paulo, Berlin or around the world following the *standard* of globalization. The meaning of urban aesthetics lies in the configuration of the image, or rather in its cultural and social aspects linked to creativity in order to understand the semantic universe of metropolitan contemporaneity in its beauty and reverse, vice versa. In this way, interventions in urban centers, through digital technology or the materialization of new ideas, for example, installations, visual arts panels or advertising, need to be analyzed in the sense of a social meaning through art and architecture. In principle, the analysis of the contemporary image in urban centers should reconsider the important works under ideological structures. Reality is, at the same time as ideology, the meanings surrounding social relations, on which the social subject can rely in order to realize itself. The orientation that Louis Althusser's classic analysis offers us in his work entitled *Sur la reproduction*[1] , after an important interpretation of Marx's theory on *Capital,* allows us to understand the modern constitution of institutional forms that orient relations, in the sense of social being, towards the configuration of the image as an expression and reference of ideological discourse. This configuration, from a theoretical point of view, implies the value of the ideal of world citizenship and cosmo-political law. It's also about the various historical forms of interpellation and existential forms in general, which are constitutive of humanity through their subjective aspects. With regard to political philosophy, for example, the importance of Hegel's work was undeniable for Karl Marx to build his theory on capital and labor, in other words, on the relations of production.

Referring to the world communication system, through the configuration of the contemporary image, we address the cultural diversity of societies that are important to urban centers. As a concept of social formation, that is, a scientific concept, a system in which we find various theories to designate societies situated in their historical time. According to Althusser, the system of ideological notions, to which the idealist notion of society refers, is to be found in production relations. This dynamic of production relations is always in development. Based on this relationship, we can highlight the dominant modes of production in order to describe contemporaneity in urban centers, defining the image to conceptualize today's society.

In the consumer society, the production of images is closely linked to the world market

---

1 Translation of the title: *On Reproduction* (reading of the work in the original French, interpreted by Christiane Wagner). ALTHUSSER, Louis. *On reproduction.* Paris: PUF, 1995.

system, in other words, to capitalism. Which, on the other hand, is integrated into this process not only through use and exchange values, according to Louis Althusser's analysis of production relations and productive forces, but also through symbolic values to give the images created a meaning in the universe of the cultural industry. This is shown by the studies of Jürgen Habermas and the aesthetic analysis of Theodor Adorno, in his work on mass society (1947) and Walter Benjamin with his essays, including *The Work of Art in the Age of Technical Reproducibility* (1935)[2] . These studies were very important for the analysis of images from the second half of the 20th century onwards. When they began to be configured and emitted unlimitedly, easily, continuously and with each new technology. Until, today, in the face of technological convergence and configured images, a possible hypothesis is found: if the world is dependent on the production of images that stimulate consumption, then it is assumed that there is an imagined world of consumerism and, therefore, that we would have an urban life that is based on nothing real. Given the importance of images in contemporary society, it is important to reflect on man's social participation through his traditional representations and/or innovations. This would enable them to understand and preserve what represents reality, without detriment to the symbolic element. In this sense, the images of today's world stimulate the desire to consume everything that is presented as reality. This is only possible because of the current technical conditions, because of the innovations, inventions and creations that allow us to foresee any imagined consequences. In this condition, the image becomes the main product of technique, that is, of the development and transformation of processes, of means becoming ends and vice versa. Thus, the production and fascination of images never cease to conditionally indicate that reality is itself imagination. This means that

2 There are four versions of The *work of art at the time of its technical reproducibility*. The first was written in 1935. In 1936, Benjamin introduced significant changes for its publication. This article, with its significant changes, was only published posthumously in 1955. In 1936, he also wrote, with the help of Pierre Klossowski, a French version of his text that was published in the *Zeitschrift für Sozialforschung*. This version was published in Walter Benjamin's writings in French (Gallimard, 1991). The fourth and last version, however, dates back to 1939. It was translated in 1959 by Maurice de Gandillac in Selected Works of Benjamin (Julliard), the translation first published *in Œuvres II. Poésie et révolution* (Denoël, coll. Les Lettres Nouvelles, 1971) and *L'Homme, le langage et la culture (Denoël-Gonthier, coll. Mediations, 1983)*. Finally, revised by Rainer Rochlitz, in *Œuvres III* (Gallimard, 2000). Another translation by Christophe Jouanlanne and Marc B. de Launay can be found in the volume *Sur l'art et la photographie* (Ed. carrée, coll. Arts et Esthétique, 1997). Éditions Allia, Paris, 2009.

everything can be represented or produced in a process made possible by technological evolution.

Based on Kantian philosophy, transcendental aesthetics is an aesthetic judgment that should be understood as a judgment about art and beauty. To clarify things further, he prefers to call it "transcendental aesthetics", i.e. the doctrine that deals with the *a priori* forms of sensible knowledge. Kant's writings on art and beauty, however, were no longer restricted to Baumgarten's doctrine. They went much further. Here we see the constructive nature of art, especially with regard to form and content. From this moment on, Kant began to conceive of aesthetic activity as a form of reflective judgment. Thus, Kant's constructive character necessarily involves meticulous analysis and observation of the artistic object, without this meaning the use of a pre-established rational logic. The best contemporary example of the constructive nature of art is precisely creative activity. Just to name a few, here are the world exhibitions with innovative proposals for urban centers. With regard to exteriorities and their contents. Not by chance, Hegel adds that we can imagine that the artist selects the best forms in the outside world and configures them, through his choice of composition, to find those most suited to their content. But when he does this, he hasn't done anything yet, because the artist must be a "creator" and, in his fantasy, with the recognition of true forms, with the deep sense and sensitivity that would give him the strength to spontaneously express the meaning with force. Along the same lines as Hegelian thought are the ideas of Hungarian philosopher Gyorgy Lukàcs (1885-1971), for whom art is a "reflection of reality". It results from the interaction between man and nature, with work and society as essential elements for the act of creation. In this way, the historical moment would be of paramount importance not only in the artist's moment of creation, but in the very aesthetic conception of his work. Thus, Lukàcs sees art as the most appropriate form of expression and a greater self-consciousness of humanity, "consciousness proper to the human race"[3] .

In the same way, works by contemporary thinkers are essential if we are to better

3 Dictionnaire des philosophes. Sous la direction de Denis Huisman. LUKÀCS, G., Paris: PUF, 2009. p. 1195.

understand the study of innovation in aesthetics and the changing images of[4] . To this end, the work of Professor Marc Jimenez[5] , from the University of *Paris 1 Panthéon-Sorbonne*, is important as a guide. No less important are the reflections of the main theoreticians of the Frankfurt School. The notion of the cultural industry, developed by Theodor Adorno and Max Horkheim in the context of the critical theory of culture, is particularly important for this research. Mainly because the configuration of the image in terms of aesthetic transformation in the environment of the cultural industry is the object of study and is understood here as the conception of the image of an environment, its aesthetic presentation in space, form and functionality. Conception and realization are closely linked to the creative profession. In fact, to put it more clearly, they are truly responsible for the outcome of a visual communication project. In this context, however, we have to think about the emergence of a contemporary aesthetic. In the visual aspect, for example, something that meets the most diverse segments of society, regardless of social class. Another aspect concerns the difficult democratic representation of beauty when this concept is thought of in terms of taste. In any case, the creative and their counterparts will all have to communicate with society in the best way possible, presenting their project in an aesthetically and symbolically up-to-date way.

The technique, as it is a means of realizing visual communication in urban centers, has become indispensable. It's a whole technique, especially with the constant evolution of this segment. It has made a significant contribution to projects in the technical improvement of visual communication in large cities, in the search for solutions for 21st century society. The literature on visual communication opens up a significant space for researchers interested in its social effects. At the same time, in view of its broad scope, some of its specialties, without prejudice to others, have been prioritized

4 There are two images. The first, understood objectively, are graphic, photographic, plastic and dynamic representations, such as the image in a photograph, printed in a magazine or newspaper, broadcast on television, on a canvas, of an artifact. The second image is subjective, the word image is understood as a memory, an impression you have of something, such as the image you have of idols, the image you have of artists. Objective images transcend borders, create and provide free access to the imagination and therefore have a place beyond the immediate social environment.

5 JIMENEZ, Marc. *Qu'est-ce que l'esthétique?* Gallimard/Folio Essais, 1997.
Id. L'esthétique contemporaine. Paris: Klincksieck, 2004.

in terms of academic research.

The object of this study is justified by the need for research, study, analysis and a better understanding of innovation in the configuration of the contemporary image. It is understood that it is not enough just to attribute the fascination that aesthetic "beauty" exerts on the individual. Not even functionality, its effective, convenient, practical or utilitarian use, explains this polysemy of the creative's work. In the same way that the work of art enshrined in architecture or the visual arts, the "beautiful" always has a multiplicity of meanings, so does the work of the designer in the configuration of his project. In this case, however, there is one aspect that needs to be considered. Unlike other artistic manifestations, the designer's "art" often has a contiguous coexistence between the object and its user. It's as if there really was an interaction, a dialog between the two. It is this kind of "reciprocal appropriation" between people and things that differentiates the work of creativity.

But what we previously called "reciprocal appropriation" is just one of the distinctive qualities inherent in the work of the creative. Apart from this aspect, other segments of the profession have multiple productive activities, which, contrary to what was previously recorded, are works contemplated by the general public, present in the creative daily life of urban centers. And here it is worth noting a very important aspect: the confluence between the work of the designer, the architect and the artist, precisely because of the close relationship that has always existed between these activities. They have always aimed to innovate in the visual arts.

One of the works that will drive thinking about innovation in contemporary society is the book *Où va le monde?*[6] by French sociologist Edgar Morin. According to him, the future is created by the action of the abstract present, which is linked to knowledge of the past. From this perspective, Edgar Morin opposes the simplistic conception that past and present are known and that the action of development is linear. There is no shortage of arguments to explain that the past contributes to knowledge of the present.

6 MORIN, Edgar. *Où va le monde ?* Paris : Éditions de L'Herne, 2007. p. 16. (Where is the world going?) Titulo trad. por Christiane Wagner.

The experiences of the present contribute to knowledge of the past in transformation, in other words, the present changes, the experiences follow each other with each new present. Thus, Morin's ideas lead us to interpret that knowledge of the present becomes essential for forming any knowledge of the future. According to Morin, this is essential for knowledge of the present. The exposition of his ideas, in this logic of reasoning, leads us to admit that the condition of contemporary creations and inventions can be imagined. Theories show that the process of creativity aims at the relationship between art and industry in its aesthetic and social aspects. With regard to studies of the cultural industry, the bibliographical support of the classics of the Frankfurt School and the contemporary writings of the French School on mass society are necessary to establish the status of the contemporary image.

The status of the contemporary image is analyzed in terms of its polysemic character, i.e. its form, the multiplicity of its meaning in contemporary society, its content, its usefulness and the technological transformations in its configuration. Based on the readings of Baudrillard's works, it can be seen that all the semiology surrounding simulacra and simulation, or even illusion, aesthetic disillusion[7] , offer meaning to the object of this research. The research is conditioned to the problem of the "true" meaning of the image. Whether it's aesthetic or innovative. The fact is that, in this image, we find reasons for contemporary reality, in line with Kantian thinking when he talks about reason. With objective definitions of the organization of the elements belonging to the process of creativity for realization, the abstraction of the configuration of images is clarified, seeking better reasons to understand the relationship between the individual and their environment. At the same time, we have to consider the manifestation of the image through imagery of all kinds, in a constant search for recognition. In his essay *Illusion, Aesthetic Disillusionment,* the theorist Baudrillard says that "nowadays, everything wants to manifest itself. Technical, industrial and media objects, artifacts of all kinds want to signify, to be seen, read, recorded and photographed."[8]

---

7 BAUDRILLARD, Jean. *Illusion, désillusion esthétiques.* France: Sens & Tonka, 1997.
8 *Ibid.*, p. 31 (cited in French translation by Christiane Wagner)

From this perspective, and in order to better emphasize the research problem, the aim is to use the imaginary of social fulfillment as a secondary foundation. For, as the author further states, if an individual thinks that it is a pleasure to want to photograph an object, it is actually the object that wants to be photographed. Information and communication technologies would be seen as responsible for shaping the environment and as means of expression, or even as a source of innovation and creativity by influencing the individual from childhood, from playful images to images in general. The same applies to the coherence and continuity of a work of art in its aesthetic and cultural aspects. Finally, it would be necessary to understand the cultural industry in its creative aspects, with the aim of combining contemporary aesthetics, in the innovation of the urban image, with a local and global market economy, in the pragmatic sense. The empirical element results from direct observation of the phenomenon of innovation, with professionals from the creative market, professors and researchers, cultural events such as exhibitions, installations, and above all the meaning of urban art, among others. The confluence of theoretical and empirical research makes it possible to understand the status of the contemporary image in its perception values through an urban aesthetic.

1. transformations of the urban image

1.1. Space, ideologies and achievements

The process of evolution meets the objectives of the individual in their development in large cities by presenting a path full of meanings in the history of civilization and social life, in relation to technological changes. Transformations are considered to be the main characteristic of an urban visual culture as representations of a conception of the world with its own characteristics and needs, which vary according to culture, society and economy. Among many achievements, this chapter will present a historical and reflective analysis of the time and space of some essential periods, comparing technical possibilities as stages in the life of the individual and one of the various processes of social reality.

Creativity is presented in its realization processes as the meaning of the urban image in its process of contemporary transformation and the reality of consumer society. In this way, Morin's thinking makes sense of the development of this study in innovation and creation as image configurators, which, as an exception to the common rule, are a characteristic that is becoming stronger as a trend in visual communication and architecture projects. Thus, the action of the present develops around the economy, technology, science, ideologies, political will, etc. These actions transform evolution and, from this perspective, we can reflect on the conditions that allow for innovation and the creation of everyday events. One of these conditions is the configuration of images that turns the exception into the general rule, transforming the predictable and everything that is seen as conventional or traditional.

In this sense, one of the consequences of technical innovation is industrial development. The production of cultural goods circulates around the world according to the logic of the global market. The logic of cultural dynamics itself encompasses knowledge, belief, art, laws, morals, customs and all social achievements. It is life in society that drives culture, as well as an individual's orientation towards building their identity and maintaining the balance of their own cultural *ethos*. Furthermore, a culture is characterized by its form of transmission, which can be understood as a tradition.

This is the condition for maintaining, over time, the wisdom of generations, their achievements and history, or rather, accepting the past in the present and preserving it in order to pass it on to the future. Among other things, in the contemporary urban context at the beginning of the 21st century. Similarly, the power of the media is marked by innovations in the configuration of images that propose ideas of vanguardism and progress. Also, in the area of knowledge, action or the creation of projects and plans, cultures represent the social *ethos* in order to meet realization, notably resulting in opinions. However, opinions drive society and, as a result, the world. So the cultural realization of the big metropolises represents the way of life of urban society. This contemporary lifestyle is based on the *media* spreading the ideas of mass society. The widespread production of images is possible in a context that is favored by the dynamics of the market itself, leading to consumption. This is because contemporary metropolises and society report and represent their stories, experiences, hopes, in short, their daily lives, through images that propose a projection as the identity of the social actor, that is, the individual acting in society. This projection transmits, for most people, the collective imagination.

Evolution leads us to urban development, an increase in the urban population and evolution in architecture. When it comes to time and space, apart from metaphysical reflections, what there is in architecture and visual communication for analyzing time and space is what concerns the arrangement of volumes in space and the relationship in terms of urban exploration. The growth of cities requires projects that can solve problems of agglomeration, visual communication and signage. Creation proposals using different techniques for urban development are the result of the late 20th century. City growth has been a phenomenon since the dawn of civilization. Time, therefore, is more related to the ability to relate the development of technique to the solution of projects that can be solved according to the growth of urban centers. The relationship between space and the transformation of the city. This is the great challenge. As time goes by, the process of changing the shape of the city implies measures to control both population growth and the decentralization of metropolitan centers. For example, the solutions found by some cities that have followed ideas from the Middle Ages, but in a form suited to contemporary times. Following the model of medieval walled cities with the center at the head, rather than at the core. Like, for example, the city of Brasilia with its government center - the Praça dos Três Poderes - with its urban planning developed by Lùcio Costa and designed by Oscar Niemeyer and inaugurated on April 21, 1960 during the presidency of Juscelino Kubitschek, has its planning, the pilot plan in the shape of an airplane. But Brasilia was designed and only then was it built. The transformation of the city is more characterized by time and the development of society. Ideas allied only to space do not correspond to the expected results for a city in constant growth, transformation and evolution.

In his study published in the book *Space, Time and Architecture - the development of a new tradition,* Sigfried Giedion presented the shape of cities in constant change. From this work, one can understand impossible ideas for solving the problems of organizing a city in constant change, such as the senseless idea of completely destroying the city in order to build a new one, as Frank Lloyd Wright wanted. A total destruction of the city would only be possible through a natural catastrophe. According to Sigfried Giedion, the conception of space does not occur independently and autonomously, but through the organization of forms in space. At any period in the history of civilization, the condition for projection is the perception of space/time by relating the volumes arranged in internal and external spaces, or the interrelationship between them. With the spaces typical of the great civilizations - such as in Egypt, the pyramids in Giza; or in Greece, the temples in Athens. What most characterized this relationship of volume in space was the unlimited breadth that shaped space. The significance of architectural form and the relationship between internal and external space is of great importance in relation to space/time, when we look at the sense of tradition in works in large spaces with vaulted roof designs.

However, we can exemplify predominant characteristics of creativity, using the same fundamental elements, in relation to space, maintaining in their time the symbolic aspects that represent tradition, but in an innovative way. Like Oscar Niemeyer's creativity in the creation of the National Congress. Let's take a look at the architect's words: "It's the same when adopting the dome - the vault that the Egyptians used and the Romans multiplied - in the building of the National Congress." For Niemeyer, the creativity was in the plastic intervention, in the modification seeking, as the architect says, "to make it lighter". The architecture of the National Congress was created with the fundamental elements, which are the two plenary halls where the decisions of the Brazilian government are made. This was therefore the criterion for its realization, as Niemeyer confirms: "giving them greater emphasis was our plastic objective, placing them on a monumental esplanade where their forms stand out as true symbols of legislative power."

Projects that allow for vaults at the highest center and also at the lowest points, whether concave or convex, are, in the perception of the individual, an image that offers the exuberance of power, as was the Baroque period, giving an imposing aspect through the symmetry of the architecture, offering optical illusions and, above all, perspective through the illusionist paintings and frescoes on the ceilings. But over time, perception transforms the same fundamental elements into new configurations, expressing its values, which are also "absolute" in their time and space. Like the modernity of Oscar Niemeyer or the high technology of Norman Foster, in translating the values that a nation idealizes.

As Giedion's studies show, today shapes, surfaces and planes not only shape the internal space, but also the limits of their own dimensions, configuring distinct volumes in the open space and making sense of the conception of contemporary architectural space. An example of this is the Reichstag in Berlin, the seat of the German parliament, which is of great importance in the country's political history and an architectural symbol for its grandeur and image of power to the world. It was designed by the architect Paul Wallot, who competed with 190 other projects in the 1882 competition to build the Parliament. After numerous changes to the project, construction began on June 9, 1884. The symbolic dome was registered when William I (Keiser Wilhelm I) was in power. On December 5, 1894, Paul Wallot completed his work. What most characterized the project as symbolic was the dome. Both in the initial design, when developed by Paul Wallot and perfected by Hermann Zimmermann due to the advanced engineering techniques of the time, using steel and glass in the construction of the dome, which measured 75m in height, over the plenary hall, offering natural lighting to the internal environment. As for the outside environment, it was a reference to symbolize Parliament, and against the wishes of William II (Keiser Wilhelms II) who obviously didn't want Parliament, even describing it in 1892 as "a kingdom of monkeys (*Reichsaffenhaus*)", "a complete and unfortunate creation (*vollig verunglückte Schopfung*)" and "a summit of bad taste (*Gipfel der Geschmacklosigkeit*)". These expressions sound like strong, heavy words in a Latin language like Portuguese, and one can even imagine the Emperor in his Germanic bearing contesting the building for Parliament. With the Reichstag completed and in the midst of the First World War in 1916, the monarchy, already weakened, ceased to exercise power over the people. And, in principle, for the ideal of a German Parliament, a banner was planned on the front portico of the Reichstag with the phrase: THE GERMAN PEOPLE, placed at the time of the fall of the monarchy and the consolidation of the Federal Republic of Germany. The letters that form this phrase in German are: D, E, M, E, U, T, S, C, H, E, N, V, O, L, K, E (*Dem deutschen Volke*). The detailed history of the meaning of this phrase is to be found in the *Bundestag* archives and in a 2010 special publication by the *Bundestag,* reporting that the company contracted in 1915 to place the letters, in bronze, was a Jewish arts company, the founder of which was Samuel Abraham Loevy. The meaning of this phrase, for the Union of German States, for a republic and democracy, also came to have more unique meanings for German Jews who formed German families by choice, like Loevy.

On February 27, 1933: four weeks after the National Socialist Party took power, the Reichstag was set on fire. With theories "configured"[9] by the power of the National Socialist Party against communism, the Nazis gained strength and strategies to destroy

9 Sven Felix Kellerhoff, in an interview for the Spezial magazine's special publication Blickpunkt Bundestag in 2010, revealed that despite all the evidence, the only perpetrator of the Reichstag fire was Marinus van der Lubbe, a communist from the Netherlands, as an act of protest. From your research, all you can find is evidence concentrated on this accusation and nothing else. No evidence yet for another "truth". But still in this interview, Kellerhoff concluded that all the ideas surrounding the supposed possibility that it was an articulation of the National Socialist Party are, above all, associated with the atrocities committed against the rights and heritage of humanity.

democracy and turn the Reichstag into a symbol for the Nazi Dictatorship. The Reichstag, from 1894 to the present day, has always been a monument of great symbolic value for the transformations that have taken place in the world. It is a reference point for the political, social and ideological evolution of the German people and the world as a whole, shaped by the events, facts and achievements that configure the collective image of urban space through the widespread use of technology and the ways in which ideologized values are transmitted and materialized by humanity itself, whether it is art or not, at first glance or over time as a narrative, through the diversity and polysemy of meanings. In 1999, the Reichstag, the seat of the Bundestag in Berlin, confirmed it as a symbolic monument for the whole world. In the technical aspects of his creative and realization processes, Paul Wallot intended at the time to develop a new national style, an architectural reference for the unification of the German states and cultural regions of the German Empire. For the external form, Wallot mainly used the forms of the Italian High Renaissance and combined them with elements of the German Renaissance in a neo-Baroque style. For the Dome, as already mentioned, he used steel and glass in the construction, which was ultra-modern for the time. The result was not seen by many critics as a successful synthesis, but as a confused work. Traditionalists rejected the dome's modern technology and young critics couldn't get used to the Renaissance style. On the frontispiece is the coat of arms of the unification of the German empires: the Federal State and the Emperor. Other reliefs are to the right and left. They show the coats of arms of each state, country and city that were unified in 1871.

Because of its symbolic meaning, William II didn't want the dome over the plenary hall. Paul Wallot made a glass and steel construction possible, techniques and materials resulting from the industrial revolution and ultra-modern at the time. It was 20 meters higher than the current dome, which is also considered a *high-tech* project, developed by the architect and designer Norman Foster, who won the competition to renovate the Reichstag.

Today, however, we find another aspect after the fall of the wall, when the German

Bundestag decided in 1991 to set up its headquarters in Berlin. Norman Foster presented a technologically advanced project that maintained the building's historic character. In total, 45,000 tons of material were extracted from the building. It wasn't until 1997, when the inside of the building was completely empty, that construction began. In 1999, the Reichstag became the symbol of a new era for the German parliament.

Space, in an abstract sense, is where evolution is found. But evolution, according to Edgar Morin, never obeys a law or even a preponderant determinism. Evolution is neither mechanical nor linear. There is no dominant factor controlling it. For Morin, the future would indeed be very simple if evolution depended on a predominant factor and a linear causality. Therefore, it would be even more meaningless if we started from a forecast based on a simplistic conception of evolution. Social reality is multidimensional. It includes demographic, economic, technical, political and ideological factors. For Morin, each of these factors can be dominant at certain times and, even in their autonomous processes, they exert a causality of their own and are subject to external determinations.

In short, inventions, innovations, creations, techniques, cultures, ideologies, emerge and modify evolution, sometimes revolutionizing it, from its principles of evolution. Innovations and creations are the exceptions to the rules, through which they can develop and strengthen trends, and be introduced into the dominant trend, modifying its orientation or even replacing it. History doesn't flow like a river, according to Morin, it develops around the norms towards a new norm. Evolution is change. Industry develops not because of previous civilization, but because of persuasion in traditional society. Thus, the evolution, time and space of the 20th century and its passage into the 21st century represented significant progress in scientific, technical, economic, industrial, socio-cultural and techno-bureaucratic development. Above all, the 20th century was marked by two major world wars, the biggest in the history of mankind. On the one hand, a century of progress and development, of a rational appearance, and on the other, marked by the horror of wars and conflicts.

The second half of the 20th century saw the start of a new economic *boom*, a process of urbanization and industrialization in Europe, Japan and the United States. It was a period marked by crisis and, from Morin's point of view, we are not only in a society in which a cultural crisis emerged in 1968 and a new economic crisis under the effects of oil enrichment that still prevail today. We are living this society's way of being, in other words, a society in crisis, at the beginning of the 21st century. *"La crise n'est pas le contraire du développement, mais sa forme même"*[10]. The idea that crisis has become our society's way of being is that development carries within itself a crisis character as its own process. The transforming and accelerating movement that development has is: economic, social and cultural disruption and disorganization. Development is inseparable from destruction and transformation based on the disorganizing and reorganizing process characteristic of crisis. The reflections of sociologist Edgar Morin focus on the individual as a social being, in all the contradictions of the representations that fragment him, especially in 21st century society. His theory provides a new vision of consumer society and urban life, in which human identity is at stake in the course of the planetary crisis. His work defends the idea of the relationship between past, present and future, discussing where this path will lead us, what the crisis means and what the old ideologies are worth in the face of the interests of the 21st century: inventions, innovations, creations, techniques, cultures, ideologies, which modify or revolutionize the principles of evolution. Initially, one of the consequences of technical innovation is industrial development. In this context, the production of cultural goods circulates around the world according to the logic of the global market. The dynamics of the world market will be analyzed in this chapter by means of cultural production. What comprises this production is knowledge, beliefs, the arts, laws, morals, custom and the sum total of social achievements. It is life in society that leads to culture, the individual's sense of being, to build their identity according to their cultural characteristics.

Among other things, in a contemporary urban environment, such as Paris or Berlin at

10 "Crisis is not the opposite of development, but its very form." (MORIN, Edgar. *Where is the world going?* Paris: L'Herne, 2007 p.32

the beginning of the 21st century, the power of the *media* has been marked by innovations in the configuration of images that propose ideas for the *avant-garde* of progress. Furthermore, in the realm of knowledge, action or the creation of projects and plans, cultures represent reality in order to bring it to fruition, notably by resulting in opinions. Thus, the sum of opinions guides society and, consequently, the world. Then there is the cultural realization of the great economic metropolises. The contemporary way of life with the support of the *media* allows ideas to spread.

The existence of the image industry's strong production may be possible in a favorable context, to such an extent that it leads to the consumption of images. Because contemporary metropolises and society tell and represent their stories and their experiences, in short, their daily lives, through images, they propose a projection of the identity of the social actor, that is, the conduct of the individual in society. A projection that conveys, for most people, the collective imagination. In addition to the diversity of television programs, audiovisuals, film production and advertising, the visual arts are also the means by which images can construct cultural identities. In this context of values intrinsic to the nation, i.e. language, tradition, art, history, etc., images are displayed in the public space with their ideologies, on the local market and then on the world market. The latter is a production in the globalized culture that is the world of exchange for fragments of identity.

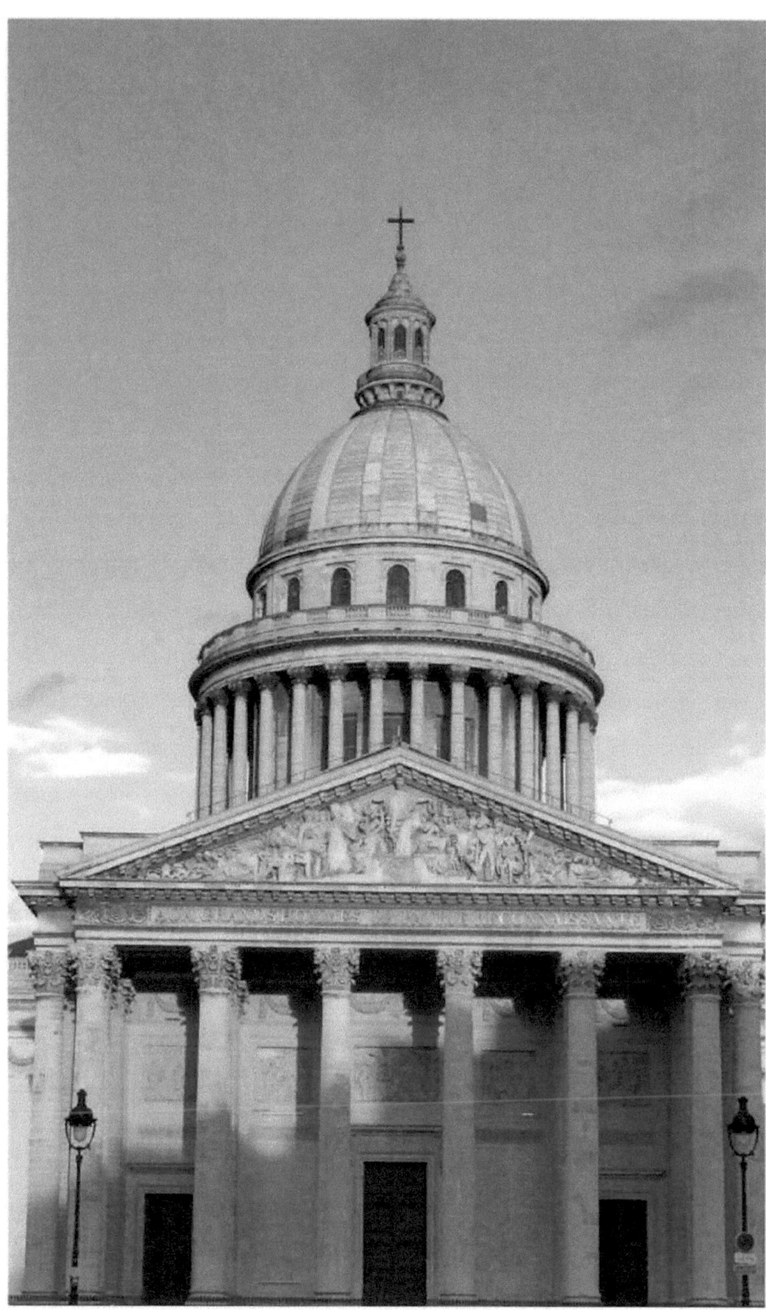

Panthéon, Paris. Photo by Christiane Wagner, 2012.

2. Industry and communication

Forms in urban space have long been observed and studied in the history of art and architecture. However, economic growth and industrialization are incisive factors in the articulations of urban expansions, which consist of the growth of cities and urbanization. The main factor in the evolution of industrialization is the modernization of its equipment. In the case of basic industries, the focus is on energy and the steel industry. As a result, market policies have led to projects for new sources of energy to replace oil or nuclear power, for example, with political clout and huge current investment. Germany, for example, ended its use of nuclear energy resources in 2011. The transformations affect the spaces and *habitats of* the population. The causes are varied and different in each city and culture. Development is always constant, at all levels, and otherwise there could be no expectation of civilization. The relationship between industry and the city is transformed, of course, by technological innovation. But these changes are always conditional on choices. So, to find out the reasons for investing in certain choices, we consulted Marcel Roncayolo's essay[11] , *Nouveau cycle* ou *fin de l'*urbanisation*?*), in which, from the author's point of view, in the best examples, it is above all a question of a strategy and rarely of an obvious determinism, by showing when the industries in their origin were located right in the capital, where they found high quality craftsmanship, as in Paris, in the best neighborhoods (Puteaux, Levallois and Neuilly). Then, in search of labor reserves or more spacious places with better conditions and also to favor exports with their assembly lines in port regions. Urbanization is not just an effect, but a cause of economic growth, and above all concerns transformations in the way of life, not just in terms of relations with the utilitarian objects of everyday life, but especially in terms of what economic growth brings in relation to changes in the conditions of collective existence. To get an idea of this growth, the reference provided by Roncayolo in France, regarding the importance of the automobile industry, considering investments in communications equipment,

---

11 RONCAYOLO, Marcel (dir.). Jacques BRUN, Guy BURGEL, Jean-Claude CAHMBOREDON, Françoise CHOAY, Michel COSTE, Jacques JULLIARD. *La ville aujourd'hui. Urban changes, decentralization and the crisis of the city. History of urban France.* Paris : Éditions du Seuil, 2001.

infrastructure, education and housing in the long term, is that in 1949, there was a growth of 36%; in 1954, 63%; and in 1966, 68%. The car is the central element in the transformation of public space and collective life and, finally, in the consequences of urbanization. With the growth in purchasing power, the capitals, and even the other cities in their process of urbanization, have not had their way of life changed by urbanization.

But rather through the relationship with space, public infrastructure and all the significant and useful objects that are produced to meet everyday needs. Therefore, with an emphasis on design, a process of planning objectivity, of strategies, which is also a function on the part of urbanization. For example, the search for alternative, non-polluting transport, through public bicycle systems, projects in partnership with designers, architects and industry in the redevelopment of cities with large flat areas, such as Paris, Lyon in France[12] or Berlin in Germany[13] , or even Sao Paulo and around the world, as we can see from *The Bike-sharing World Map* .[14]

The utopia of many urban planners and architects that their concepts would change ways of life is found in many creative projects. However, the reality consists of the concrete and plausible facts that urbanization does not create ways of life, but offers support for the possibilities of some models that meet the expectations of public life. Urbanization, design and architecture projects that address social reality focus on the problems generated by it. For example, the implementation of the public bicycle system in 2007 in the city of Paris, by agreement between the City Council and the company JCDecaux (la Mairie de Paris et JCDecaux), which was revised in 2009 due to problems not foreseen in the initial budget for maintenance and the viability of continuing the service. [15] The complexity of these problems encompasses production, consumption, the city, the habits of citizens in the rhythm of their lives amidst their most diverse values. Among so many criteria that classify the citizen through their

---

12 Available at: <http://www.velib.paris.fr/> . Accessed on: 11/03/2012.
13 Available at: <http://www.nextbike.de/> and also at: <http://www.callabike- interaktiv.de/>. Accessed on: 11/03/2012.
14 Available at: <http://bike-sharing.blogspot.com> and also at : <http://www.metrobike.net/>. Accessed on: 11/03/2012.
15 *Some Vélib users have a case against JC Decaux.*
Article published in : <http://www.lefigaro.fr/actualite-france/2010/12/20>.
Accessed on 11/03/2012.

cultural background and education (*Bildung*), consequently, their choices, habits and taste, when we consider the bicycle in its technical and aesthetic configuration as a result of Patrick Jouin's project[16] . This complex relationship, analyzed by Edgar Morin, means that we must always consider some particular data in relation to the totality of which they are part, as well as the totality in relation to the parts. Morin also makes it clear that we need to unify our assessment and place the object of study in its context and complexity. The problems of our civilization are the consequences of this complexity, which consists of technical, economic and industrial development. These factors imply an increase in needs, production and consumption, above all, in contemporary times, the saturation of energy resources due to constant consumption. From economic growth we come to ecology. A theme that leads the world from the end of the 20th century to the present day, in projects and the use of new forms of energy as a new path for society towards a civilization from the 21st century onwards, under a political context. The *polis* and cultural diversity have come to the fore since the major world conferences, with the aim of leading the world down a different path, shaping the image with elements that characterize this complex reality of consumption, pollution, global warming and all the threats to the human species.

In 1992, heads of state and government from all over the world, meeting in Rio de Janeiro, approved by 'consensus' [let's use the word consensus here to analyze Jürgen Habermas' theory of the rational practice of communication in discursive evaluation - *Geltungsansprüche*] a set of principles that aimed to lay new foundations for the production and distribution of the wealth generated by human work, that contemplated the appropriate use of the resources offered by the planet and ensured that everyone had the right to live with dignity, both in the present and in the future. The document, known as Agenda 21, points the way and defines the responsibilities of each social

16 For the city of Paris, JCDecaux has proposed a bicycle designed around a specification defined by the study office in keeping with the delicate balance between aesthetics and durability, ergonomics and comfort, perfect safety and impeccable service. The design allows for an apparent absence of cables and a 100% open frame of minimal length. The pearl mouse grey color, proposed by Patrick Jouin and chosen by Bertrand Delanoe, allows for a combination of elegance and harmonious integration into the urban environment. The curves that flow from the bike are convenient for the user and offer a feeling of confidence and security. The bicycle combines artistry and safety, technique and service. (Article translated by Christiane Wagner.) Source: Observeur du Design 2008 / Velib', JCDecaux SA, designer: Patrick Jouin. Available at: <http://www.designaparis.com>, accessed on 11/03/2011.

agent in the search for sustainable development, throughout its 40 chapters. One of them, in particular, deals directly with the role of industry in this process. It starts from the recognition of its decisive importance in promoting the economic and social development of each country. Ten years later, a new World Summit on Sustainable Development in Johannesburg had the opportunity to assess how much progress had been made during this period. For the Brazilian industry[17] , it is time to reflect on its actions in the search for socio-economic and environmental sustainability, as well as in the fight against poverty and the inequalities that weaken Brazilian society. The discussion of responses to supposed ecological threats has been taking place on the world stage since the 1980s, from the various conferences in Canada and Sweden on climate change to the major ones mentioned above, representing an international commitment to global responsibility on the part of each country to reduce pollutants, i.e. greenhouse gases. These discussions were only negotiated in 1997 in Kyoto, Japan. In that same year and place, on December 11, a document was drawn up, the opening of the Kyoto Protocol, to be signed by the countries that agree to the international treaty of commitments to reduce greenhouse gas emissions, which has been scientifically proven. The protocol was ratified on March 15, 1999, which implies a reform in economic activities involving a dynamic of international cooperation. But without delving into the political implications of this international relationship, we can see not only the effects of pollutants, energy depletion, waste, and all the consequences of the degradation of urban life, but also the utopias that make up fictions of a future.

The Kyoto Protocol is established by the United Nations Convention[18] on Climate Change. It consists of 28 articles and an annex, listing greenhouse gases, sectors and resource categories such as energy, industrial procedures, the use of solvents and other products for agriculture and waste. There is also a list of countries and their emission

17 *Sustainable industry in Brazil, Agenda 21*, scenarios and perspectives. Brasilia: Confederaçâo Nacional da Indústria - CNI, 2002 (Book on *World Forum - Sustainable Development* - Johannesburg - ISBN 8588566281). Developed by Christiane Wagner for Art Style Comunicação e Design in partnership with the National Confederation of Industry - CNI, ECOM Ecologia e Comunicação, UPET/Núcleo de Informação, ASCOM/Assessoria de Comunicação Social and in Johannesburg, South Africa with The Bureau Printing. *Keywords:* Sustainability, industry, economy and environment. ISSN/ISBN: 85-88566-28-1.

18 *Kyoto Protocol to the United Nations Convention on Climate Change.* Available at: < http://unfccc.int>. Accessed on: 07/03/2012.

limit or reduction targets. The main target, in view of their total reductions in their gas emissions, was less than 5% compared to 1990 and over a commitment period from 2008 to 2012. And so it is understood by the United Nations Convention on Climate Change, adopted in New York on May 9, 1992, and guided by Article 3 of the Convention, dealt with from the application of the Berlin Mandate, adopted by the Conference of Parties to the Convention at its first session.

In short, with the results discussed in Durban in 2011, other conventions were established, until then the most recent conventions, such as COP 21, against climate change. This agreement was approved by 195 nations in Paris on December 12, 2015 to initiate measures and investments for a flexible, sustainable and low-carbon future and focused on achieving long-term goals by 2050: *"Outcome of the work of the Ad Hoc Working Group on Long-term Cooperative Action under the Convention"*[19] , followed mainly by: *"Establishment of an Ad Hoc Working Group on the Durban Platform for Enhanced Action*[20] " as per note 5:

"Also decides that the Ad Hoc Working Group on the Durban Platform for Enhanced Action shall plan its work in the first half of 2012, including, inter alia, on mitigation, adaptation, finance, technology development [innovation] *and transfer, transparency of action, and support and capacitybuilding, drawing* [configurations] *upon submissions from Parties* [consensus] 21 *and relevant technical, social and economic information and expertise;*[21]

However, the issues of life and its new guidelines focus on the problems of urbanization as they relate to metropolises, their overpopulation, customs, transport and housing. Important aspects of development have already been discussed at length and have formed part of the narratives of everyday urban life as they are realized in urban centers. These achievements, inscribed in the urban dynamic and decisive for

19 *Result of the work of the Ad Hoc Working Group on Long-term Cooperation in Action under the Convention. (Excerpt translated by Christiane Wagner). Available at: <http://unfccc.int>. Accessed on: 07/03/2012.*

20 *Establishment of an Ad Hoc Working Group on the improved Durban Platform for Action (Excerpt translated by Christiane Wagner). Available at: <http://unfccc.int>, Accessed on: 07/03/2012.*

21 *It also decides that the Ad Hoc Working Group on the Durban Platform for Action to strengthen action in planning its work in the first half of 2012, including, inter alia, mitigation, adaptation, finance, technological development and technology transfers [innovation], transparency of action, support and capacity building, elaboration [configurations] through submissions by the parties [consensus] and relevant technical, economic, social information and knowledge. (Translated from English into Portuguese by Christiane Wagner). Available at: <http://unfccc.int>. Accessed on: 07/03/2012.*

transformations, centralize all power. Whether it's religion or politics, science or technology, guided by capital and narrated by artistic creations and transmitted by communication throughout the process of urbanization. In April 2011 in Berlin, the public space was full of advertisements from the main Norwegian suppliers of oil energy to Germany. However, in view of the new requirements and security measures adopted by Germany, on November 1, 2011, the official Norwegian website[22] announced that the German-Norwegian partnership had broken down. Germany is seeking to achieve the targets set for 2050, as are the other countries committed to the Kyoto Protocol and the long-term conventions revised and established in November 2011 in Durban. On the other hand, we can also see RWE's advertising of the urbanization process in Berlin in the same period. At the main points of reform in the city, associating the measures of a new international policy with the processes of urbanization.

Therefore, for the sense observed here, of the configuration of the urban image in contemporaneity, designating time and its relationship with space, it is possible to reflect the sense of evolution and perception of the individual in relation to the new interventions related to communication technologies in sync with the urban rhythm that enable images and new dimensions of spaces for an ecological future based on sustainable industry and fair trade.

In this sense, the 32ª Bienal de Sâo Paulo, held in 2016 at the Ciccillo Matarazzo Pavilion, Ibirapuera Park, Sâo Paulo, under the curatorship of Jochen Volz, presented works related to environmental issues. However, the 32ndª Bienal de Sâo Paulo, in dealing with the collectivity in relation to the very condition of our lives, sought solutions, in an optimistic way, even though the suggested theme, *Living Uncertainty*, would lead us to insecurity. The exhibition offered works commissioned in response to the transformations in which we live. These works offered the public an aesthetic

22 *Namensartikel von Bundesminister für Wirtschaft und Technologie, Dr. Philipp Rδsler, und Norwegens Ol- und Energieminister Ola Borten Moe. Available at: <http://www.norwegen.no/News and events/germany/business/Deutsch-norwegische- Energiepartnerschaft-wird-ausgebaut/ >. Accessed on: 01/11/2011.*

experience of our environment. But an environment perceived in a different way, in its vital condition for the continuity of our system in relation to urban space.

The exhibition was held inside the pavilion and integrated with the outside, which is Ibirapuera Park, designed by architect Oscar Niemeyer. The integration of these spaces aims to broaden the sense of public space through art. This integration has allowed the community to interact through art in relation to urban space, the environment and ecology.

Among the works on show were *Floresta (Forest*), sculptures by Frans Krajcberg and the project *Restauro* (2016) by Jorge Menna Barreto, which deals with farming in terms of environmental transformations, eating habits and their relationship with the environment and bio-diversity. As for the work of the artist Jonathas de Andrade, the film *O peixe* (2016) stood out for its narrative of the daily lives of fishermen in Alagoas and traditional fishing. However, the main subject of this artist's work is late modernity in the Latin American context in relation to the lack of a sense of ideology that so marked modern art, in other words, he discusses the end of utopias in his work. However, among his other works, it is worth mentioning *Selva Juridica*, co-authored by Paulo Tavares and Ursula Biemann, which deals with human rights.

"Selva Juridica" is based on research carried out on the frontiers of the Ecuadorian rainforest, in the transition between the Amazon floodplains and the Andes mountain range. This border zone is one of the most biodiverse and resource-rich regions on the planet, and is currently under pressure from the drastic expansion of large-scale mineral and oil extraction activities. Guiding the book are a series of historical legal cases that bring the forest and its indigenous leaders, lawyers and scientists to court, including one such paradigmatic case, in which the Sarayaku people recently won their case, arguing for the centrality of the "Living Forest" in the cosmology, way of being and ecological survival of their community. In these conflicts, nature no longer appears as the scene of political disputes, but as a subject endowed with rights in its own terms." (Research for Forest Law: 2014)

Today, aesthetics is still an ideal of beauty. But not as it used to be, under the gaze of the critics and theoreticians of the art world. But as a contemporary ideal of pleasure in art in relation to everyday values and urban space. Starting from its original craft - the world of poetry, paintings and sculptures - aesthetics has undergone a transformation of values and also of artistic practice. It has thus become - and according to the ethics of each culture - an experience and reflection on pleasure, through art between nature and culture and through visual arts realizations that offer meaning to today's everyday life in urban spaces.

3. Tradition and contemporary ideas

Political and social transformations are recorded mainly through works of art in public spaces. Contemporary artists have created a new way of looking and perceiving. In visual culture, the meaning of art and its interventions are important for society and its evolution. This phenomenon is full of meanings in the history of civilization, in social life, in relation to technological changes and the objectives of individuals in their development in large cities. In Berlin, we saw the importance of the Reichstag in the transition from monarchy to republic, from William II, Bismark to the present day, with Angela Merkel. In Sao Paulo, the main characteristics of a new world city are the relationship between verticalization and urbanization. On the other hand, in the old world, in France, in Paris, many artistic realizations and manifestations have marked the entire existence of that city. Especially in relation to the time and space of some important periods for French cultural transformation, such as its Revolution (1789-1799), the fall of the Monarchy and the advent of the Republic. This shows the possibilities of contemporary art gaining notoriety for its polemical aspects, with revolutionary pretexts of a cultural and aesthetic nature in the construction of the social imagination. From France to France, and from France to the world. The architectural spaces of the Château de Versailles are thus not only part of a historical moment, but a means of countering cultural values in the development of new ways of exploring space. Consequently, only through a transformative result would art be perceived today as a cultural reality.

All world issues are part of cultures, in relation to the past and innovation. So, in the dimension of the real world, realization and space, in relation to their historical marks, are the result of technological and social evolution.

During the 20th century, many researchers studied the consequences of innovations as important and necessary in the areas of technical, political and material cultures of everyday life. Today, however, the consumer society, urban life, from the point of view of sociologist Edgar Morin, is defined by the idea of the relationship between past, present and future. But in such a way that it conditions society to question where this path will lead us, what the current crisis means and what the old ideologies are worth in the face of the interests of the 21st century: inventions, innovations, creations, techniques, cultures, ideologies that modify evolution or revolutionize the principles of evolution. In this way, Morin's thinking makes sense of an analysis of this subject in terms of innovation as a configurator of images, which are the exception to the common rule, in a way, in contemporary art. A characteristic that is becoming stronger as a trend in the visual arts and that, in its relationship with everyday life, through exhibitions, also interferes with the urbanization of large centers.

Let's go back to the Renaissance for a moment, to emphasize the value of this period, in which the image of a reforming citizen who transforms time is shaped. In Wilfried Koch's book, *Kleine Stilkunde der Baukunst*, the awareness of the humanist-educated bourgeois is attested to in the construction of residences and municipal buildings, replacing ecclesiastical works as a source of culture. The classical order is valued, with the use of ribbed vaulting, with imposing vaulted arches, the ogival arch of the Gothic period gives way to the full-round arch, and the porticoes and pediments reconfigure the façades. Compared to the Reichstag, and based on the criticism presented, we can see from the theoretical work of Wilfried Koch[23] , that the criticism of the style employed by Paul Wallot is mainly due to the lack of knowledge of German architects in renovation projects like the Italians; many of them had never even seen Italy or the buildings in the ancient classical or Renaissance style. With the Baroque, reform was favored in Germany and would become, for 150 years, a model of life that took over Europe, all the elements of the Renaissance reappearing in extreme representation, in which the domes achieved great grandeur and the façades became more important. The Baroque style was very popular with absolute monarchs, especially in palaces, castles and parks of gigantic dimensions. This style is integrated throughout the architecture with sculpture, painting, music, furniture, clothing, literature, hairstyles and the way people express themselves. But because of the reactionary reactions to the splendor of the nobility, those deprived of such luxury and wealth became revolutionaries seeking

23 KOCH, Wilfried. *Kleine Stilkunde der Baukunst.* München: Mosaik, 1985.

the ideals of the Enlightenment, in critical theories of society and, like France, putting an end to the Baroque with the Revolution. Paris, still during the late Baroque period, was already in the context of a decadent monarchy under Louis XV and Louis XVI. With the predominance of rationalism, the Enlightenment strengthened political and economic actions for the Revolution of 1789. The objectivity and intellectuality of the Enlightenment was more accepted by neoclassical works, which characterized *mimesis* by imitating antiquity. One example is the Pantheon in Paris, designed by the architects Jacques-Germain Soufflot and Jean-Baptiste Rondelet. It was built between 1758 and 1790: a centralized Greek cross building with a porch of Corinthian columns, a crossing dome and columns around the drum, cross boats with a barrel vault, crowned with four smaller domes. What most characterizes the French Baroque is the use of the architectural forms of classicism, in the spirit of the Renaissance, in its outstanding grandeur, with the Château de Versailles, characterized more by the construction of castles than churches.

Today, however, the spaces consecrated as historical monuments and preserved by UNESCO remain in time, conferring the heritage of a tradition on conservatives. And to those who seek innovation through modernity, starting with the Liberty style in England (1834-1896) through the humanization of urban space through art, with William Morris, who sought unity between architecture, painting, sculpture and decorative arts as a global work. Modern architecture, using new materials due to new technologies as a result of the Industrial Revolution, used concrete, glass and iron frames. Innovation emerged, and the 20th century shaped a new image and theories about aesthetics and the search for functionality, combining industry with the daily life of the metropolis with the ever-present phrase: form follows function. So, combining public space and power, for the word "form", we can understand "configuration" as function, being the image of innovation and strategy. Therefore, all contemporary values seek in their configurations the image that can characterize values. It remains to be seen what "truth" or illusion exists in each of these realizations in their time and social reality. When it comes to the contrast between many projects that coexist with works from previous eras, the analysis is much more complex, even when it comes to urban planning. For example, the simplest and most absurd solution is to destroy cities in order to create new spaces, as Frank Lloyd Wright wanted. However, for innovative projects, others have had the chance to find almost a destruction, but an evacuation of area, for the construction of a planned city, as happened with Brasilia, by Lúcio Costa and Oscar Niemeyer, which was a possible achievement and favored by the political and social moment in which Brazil lived. In addition, of course, to the extensive area. Other reasons favor innovative works in the current space in relation to time - contemporaneity. For example, catastrophes that result in destruction transform something from the past into innovative projects, such as the Reichstag dome, which was burned down and, by consensus, rebuilt, but with new features. This is hardly ever the case when the majority defends the old. As with many cities and monuments, rebuilt after wars and maintaining their traditional values without change. On the other hand, a new space, with a lot of area, without contrasts with civilization and living with primitive people, finds a full and rich development, presenting new creations freely and uncompromisingly with the canons of antiquity. Innovation depends on a consensus of those who have the power to decide and approve the new proposals. Currently, in São Paulo, we see the projects of Decio Tozzi, an architect who stands out for his projects, praised by Oscar Niemeyer when he said that they have quality because of "the courage to adopt the new solution that intimidates so many", and, in Niemeyer's words, "that intimidates so many and is undoubtedly more difficult to conceive and elaborate"[24] . Take, for example, the importance of public park projects, especially for the city of São Paulo. Villa Lobos, designed by Decio Tozzi at the end of the 1980s, shows Niemeyer's confirmed characteristics in its extensive area, which continue to be evident in its implementation process. Especially the most recent work, in which he pays tribute to the former first lady of Brazil, Ruth Cardoso, wife of former president Fernando Henrique Cardoso, with an orchid garden. According to the architect, who also worked with the shapes of the vault, using high technology, steel and glass, the design is reminiscent of the dwellings of African, indigenous and pre-Columbian cultures, which sought both protection and constant lighting and

24 Available at: <http://www.deciotozzi.com.br/>. Accessed on 12/03/2012.

ventilation. The architect calls it "oca diàfana". Decio makes the most of his work by integrating the arts and urban space. Here is an example of the unification of the arts with the panels by the artist Claudio Tozzi, illustrating the characteristic passages of the buildings and avenues of the city of Sao Paulo.

The urban space, especially the public one, becomes a gallery when it displays the works of the artist Claudio Tozzi, offering the image of a configuration in color, contrasting with the skyscrapers of the metropolis, standing out from the other artists on the São Paulo scene to the world, as the sociologist Caldas confirms:

"His work, however, is not limited to our country. Claudio Tozzi has already shown his work abroad at the Venice, Paris, Medellin, Havana, Mexico and Gelsenkirchen Biennales in Germany. In other words, he is no longer just a national artist. [...] This is an important publication [the book on the artist's work] not only for researchers of the plastic arts, but also for scholars of Brazilian culture."[25]

25 CALDAS, Waldenyr. *The revolutionary traits in the work of artist ClaudioTozzi*. O Estado de Sao Paulo, p. 5-5, February 26, 2006.

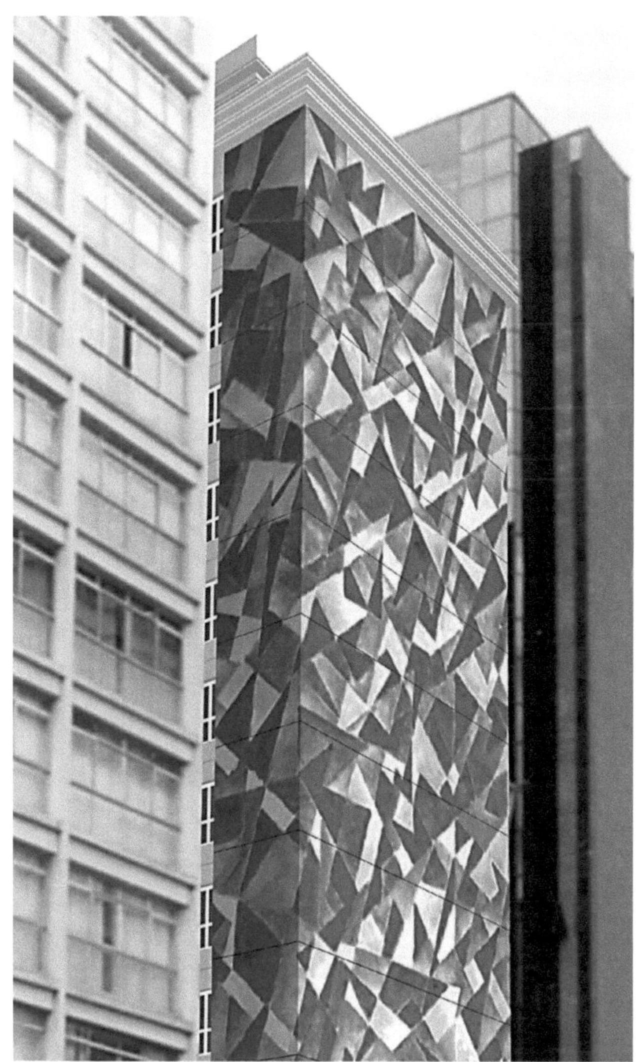

Claudio Tozzi, *Exclusive Building,* 2003

Glass mosaic $600m^2$

Urban territories, architecture, cities and their multiple interpretations have always been predominant in his work as a whole, in relation to space and time in the imagination of São Paulo citizens amidst the reality of the verticalized daily life of the city of São Paulo.

However, another reality can be found in contemporary art in France, most notably in

Paris. The scene of major social, political and artistic transformations and a reference point for the world. Even today, always part of the main themes in the world of the arts, I return to the setting of the Château de Versailles as an architectural work of great historical importance and the exhibition of Bernar Venet's sculptures that configured the image of the castle with two rows of eight arches 22 meters high. The highlight was the work installed outside the entrance gates in which, according to Venet, the sculpture is not a parenthesis, but a framing of the equestrian statue of Louis XIV in the foreground and the castle in the background. The artist installed six steel works in the gardens, also with arches of indeterminate or vertical lines. To find out more, visit the Versailles website and Dominique Poiret's article for the newspaper *Liberation* .[26]

The discussion of the ancients versus the moderns is invariably a constant subject, with little originality in the history of art. With each new exhibition or new image to be speculated on, the antagonism between old and new, tradition and progress are nothing more than a simple image of appearances. Especially in contemporary art, as Marc Jimenez explains: "*The postmodern avatar does not enter into the game of the simple duality between the past and the future. Il est le présent d'une troisième dimension, celle du métissage généralisé, de l'étendue - et non plus de la temporalité*"[27] , with reference to a previous exhibition, also controversial, at the Château de Versailles, by Takashi Murakami, one of the *stars of* contemporary Japanese art - and not the temporality - of this *show* more than 40 years *ago*, mentioned by Guy Debord, still according to Jimenez, as the moment when commodities occupy the space of social life. During Murakami's exhibition, *Le Monde* published an essay on the subject[28] by Marc Jimenez, a philosopher specializing in aesthetics and a Germanist at the Université Paris I Panthéon Sorbonne and author of *La Querelle de l'art contemporain*[29] (The discussion of contemporary art), an important work that clarifies

---

26 Available at: <http://next.liberation.fr/arts/01012339960-bernar-venet-les-arcs-de-la- discorde-a-versailles>. Accessed on: 27/05/2011.

27 (it is the avatar of post-modernism and, in addition to the simple game of duality between the past and the future, it is also the third dimension of generalized miscegenation). WAGNER, Christiane. *In visual culture, the meaning of art and its interventions.* Leaf Magazine, Brazil, p. 86-89, October 10, 2011.

28 Available at < http://www.lemonde.fr/idees/ensemble/2010/10/01/murakami-a-versailles-audace-ou-sacrilege 1418732 3232.html> . Accessed on: 01/10/2010.

29 JIMENEZ, Marc. *La querelle de l'art contemporain*. Paris, Gallimard, Folio Essais, 2005.

the meaning of contemporary art in its entirety. Finally, two years before Takashi Murakami, Versailles also received works by Jeff Koons for its Château installations. While still on the public stage, the relationship between tradition and the new ways of perceiving the symbolic universe surprises everyday life with its monumental objects by making a story. The narrative of everyday life conveyed an experience in urban space in Berlin in 1995, when the artist couple Christo and Jeanne Claude attracted millions of visitors by covering the Reichstag. Further marking this symbol with the predominant feature of the *high-tech* reconstruction of the dome.

Forms and content in urban space are such common subjects explored by the *media* from time to time on contemporary art, in France, Sao Paulo, Berlin or around the world following the *standard* of globalization. The meaning of urban aesthetics lies in the configuration of the image, or rather in its cultural and social aspects linked to creativity in order to understand the semantic universe of metropolitan contemporaneity in its beauty and reverse, vice versa. In this way, interventions in urban centers, through digital technology or the materialization of new ideas, for example, installations, visual arts panels or advertising, need to be analyzed in the sense of a social meaning through art and architecture. A new image, claiming to be innovative, would condition the aesthetic difference not only between the models and new conceptions, but also, and especially, the difference in social class in their respective regions and/or metropolises. The subtleties of stylization, the configuration of the image in relation to current technology and colors according to trends are intended to be innovative, like other elements that involve visual communication projects. As well as the difference between social classes. At this point, the creative repertoire of image making comes up against its professional condition and the challenges of new projects. Political and ideological issues aside, it would seem likely that this professional, with his creative power, could design visual communication without the redundancy of its characters, aesthetics and quality being differentiated. But the force of the stratification of consumption and the internal logic of exchange relations weighs more heavily. The purchasing power that differentiates social classes in order to maintain society's equilibrium weighs heavily. It is in this sense that research and analysis of image configuration has its practical, empirical significance in the daily life of society, specifically in visual design due to its importance in solutions for communication and signage systems in large cities. We know that nowadays visual design is essential to social representation, for communication with focused objectives, interrelationships and expected results. In short, an understanding of the condition of the globalization of culture is indispensable to any reflection on the fate of the world's cultures in the face of globalization, the flow of industrialized cultural goods, with attention to the development of new forms and functions as a specificity of an innovation in the configuration of the contemporary image in large metropolises. The way of life of urban society today, due to the representativeness that urban centers have in their image production in the configuration of the standard image, is that of the cosmopolitan image. This standard image influences the evolution of ideas and new configurations exposed to public space with their respective ideologies of the internal market and then the world market. The latter is the production of a globalized culture, which corresponds to the world of exchange of identity fragments. In contemporary times, the image we form of the city as it transforms is not just one of movement and speed, but of all the achievements that seek to continue tradition. A tradition that, because it is constantly being updated, in other words, as Morin observed, is persuaded by innovation, changes and leads society to evolve. The relationship of elements with the past, the present and ideals of a future are considered as means for the perception and imagination of contemporary expression, translated and reproduced in architectural and visual works through art and communication.

Regardless of how it is realized, the important thing is that these are the motives that condition the actions of individuals, transforming the social environment into a "flexible space", segmented from a marketing point of view. The "flexible space"[30] can be found between two poles: that of continuity and that of innovation; according to the orientation of the political-economic scenario, this "space" obtains various forms and

30 Flexible space is a conceptualization of space and time in relation to innovation. In this work, it is presented only as a complement to an evolving line of reasoning. This reasoning has its origins in the following work: WAGNER, Christiane. *In Art - invention and artifice.* São Paulo: Blücher, 2009.

possibilities of presentation, of positioning the "re-creations" in their innovative and continuity aspects. Satisfactory results are achieved, with great success for individuals or the community, when they are able to find themselves, to be in tune with this "flexible space", because this harmony generates influence, continuity and sustainment of images that illustrate the world, meeting desires and needs, or rather, "re-creating" means of wanting or needing.

An important characteristic differentiates us as *homo sapiens* within the animal kingdom and, nowadays, indicates artificial intelligence and the possible coexistence of humans and machines. Throughout our lives in society, in different cultures, we acquire and create infinite symbols that have a single importance: to give meaning to our experiences and our behavior. We thus become accepted individuals in a given culture, community or social environment, because we fit in with the standards of the environment we frequent. Above all, it's about the socio-cultural context in which the individual lives and gives meaning to life, within organized systems governed by cultural standards.

It's the capitalist system setting standards for experiences and behavior, in which the individual finds himself, looking for and creating symbols that give meaning to his existence in this capitalist system that presents itself as a flexible space in its form. Only with great skill and sensitivity would it be possible to adapt to the various forms it contains. They are the signs of the object for the desired effects, or their respective interpretants, building an innovative continuity as time goes by. Shaping the world means interpreting it with each new message. Continuity and innovation are the form of communication through inventions and artifices, opening up the possibility of different readings, each predisposed by its own ideology. The knowledge and experiences of each individual, which relate solely to the particular conditions of their life, upbringing and subjectivity, are presented as "truth" in part of a lifetime, that is, as an interpreted form of the world, absorbed and shared in their cultural environment. There is an exchange of values as a social relationship, constantly processed, in which the individual is the partial view of the world with each new message because he renews his knowledge and experiences which acquire new values. The message is born for political and economic reasons, structuring culture. All aspects of culture can be seen as communicational processes, as acquired experience, while the new element acquires meaning for invention and artifice by ideology. The new messages are on the path to this meaning, constructed in the "flexible space" between the opposing poles of continuity and innovation. If, on the one hand, Jean Baudrillard states that where we think information produces meaning, the opposite is true, he observes that the sender is the receiver in a situation where communication is annulled from the subject and not annulled from the cause, the latter still remaining without defined authorship, but of collective authorship, of cause and effect of sending and receiving messages and content. There are no two sides; there is one space and everything moves in it, in a constant exchange of the cultural sign by the collective unconscious in search of the new.

The new message, through invention and artifice, is made up of the meanings of cultural elements. Analyzing the difference between signifiers and signifieds makes it difficult to discern what can actually be considered a new message. The new message almost always conditions us to illusion, on the threshold of what Walter Benjamin called the "aura", the values that we transport from an origin to a reproduction, adding values that belong to other eras, experiences and moments in social and private history. It can also be understood that Baudrillard's simulacrum itself is the collective reproduction under Benjamin's "aura", constituting the circumstances that influence the communication process. The new message is first demonstrated by a metaphysical sense; then, looking for a signifier with connotations of meaning, the *a priori* hypothesis is codified by the verification of a new message, which is only the extension of a complete artificial language, the product of technology. It can therefore be seen that the more ramified the forms of communication, the more reproducibility there is in all dimensions, the more possibilities there are for inventions and artifices, which are always expanding, structuring decodings in different fields of influence. However, the possibility of theoretically defining the "new message" is non-existent as long as life in society exists, because there will always be continuity. It is an empirical fact as a continuous adventure, showing that curiosity prevails and the need to see the world with the help of scientific methodology, in order to better organize a circumstance of communication, experienced at this historical moment. Reflections on the backstage of the production system, the search for innovation, change and the constant desire to give new meanings are only seen as the realization of a new paradigm, which really puts us in a new condition. It breaks away from time, breaks the chain of reproducibility, destroying without eliminating. The same elements that make up the content of the media remain, but you can't be among them to make the new paradigm emerge.

It's one thing to compare the quality of life that society had in relation to technologies a century ago, or even in more distant times, with the current and possible quality of life when planning for the future. Another is to compare the production methods of each era and the different economies. Another, and one that I consider to be absolute, is to analyze the meaning of productivity, which is the only one at all times in all places, regardless of which economic or political system you belong to. It is an abstract and rational analysis, like mathematics, in which the individual is included, removed or reproduced (added, subtracted and multiplied) in its organization (by the order of the factors) and the meaning, which is the motivating origin, does not change (the result does not change).

As has already been discussed, the search for truth shows that the need to be integral is intrinsic to the individual, as if something were always missing, undefined by ignorance and, most of the time, confused by the condition of "established truth". Throughout history, the very search for knowledge has also been a search for "truth" in its various interpretations in relation to time and space, according to the Kantian argument which, in principle, was analyzed from the point of view of the individual's activity, above all, called in *In Art: invention and artifice* (Wagner, C. 2009), as a "re-creator", and by his study of the categories of understanding, from the *Critique of Pure Reason* (Kant, 1790) based on the origins of logical thought in Western philosophy. The goal of finding things of much greater value or new discoveries through the wisdom of science is to ignore the solution as the conclusion. The solution itself is a conditioner of anti-innovation, which limits invention and artifice. The pleasure is in venturing into knowledge to find new things. Wisdom is for those who think, not for those who believe in results. Because results are for those who seek them, and those who seek them are already bound by preconceptions, ideals and objectives by induction. And those who think are free to imagine new possibilities at the moment of discovery. *Eureka* - increasing humanity's life expectancy. There are certain questions that are simply outside the scientific realm.

We are unable to formulate many of the questions, let alone all the answers. The main objective is the constant search for inventions and artifices for man to build his image with his ideal of "perfection" for his life - *in Art.*

The importance of man as a creative being, more specifically the "re-creator", is the ability to create fantastic images that lead to fascination without often offering a clear interpretation of their meaning. Ambiguity can be extremely useful when implying without proving, when suggesting without defining. The new message is always linked to time, to the tribulations of life, always in a constant process of renewal; therefore, a new message is always expected. The same content is susceptible to different interpretations, always conveys a new message and leads its followers to speculation or obsession with imagination. Of course, it is known that "true perfection", rational perfection, is impossible to achieve. The important thing is the process of continuous improvement. It's taking part in the ritual of discovery. The dichotomy of the imaginary worldview and the real world is imbued with all its positive and negative aspects. Constant creation, "re-creation", through inventions and artifices is the link in this chain, it will always be the constant new message that will maintain the continuous relationship of our existence - communication during our lifetime and that of future generations. In short, "continuity and innovation" presents the broad idea that it's not the infinity of "re-creations" to be carried out, but always the continuity of the production of our messages, simulated and disguised, which give meaning to our ways of life; not the infinity of "re-creations", but the growth of possibilities, which are summed up in the only meaning, which is not argument, but invention and artifice.

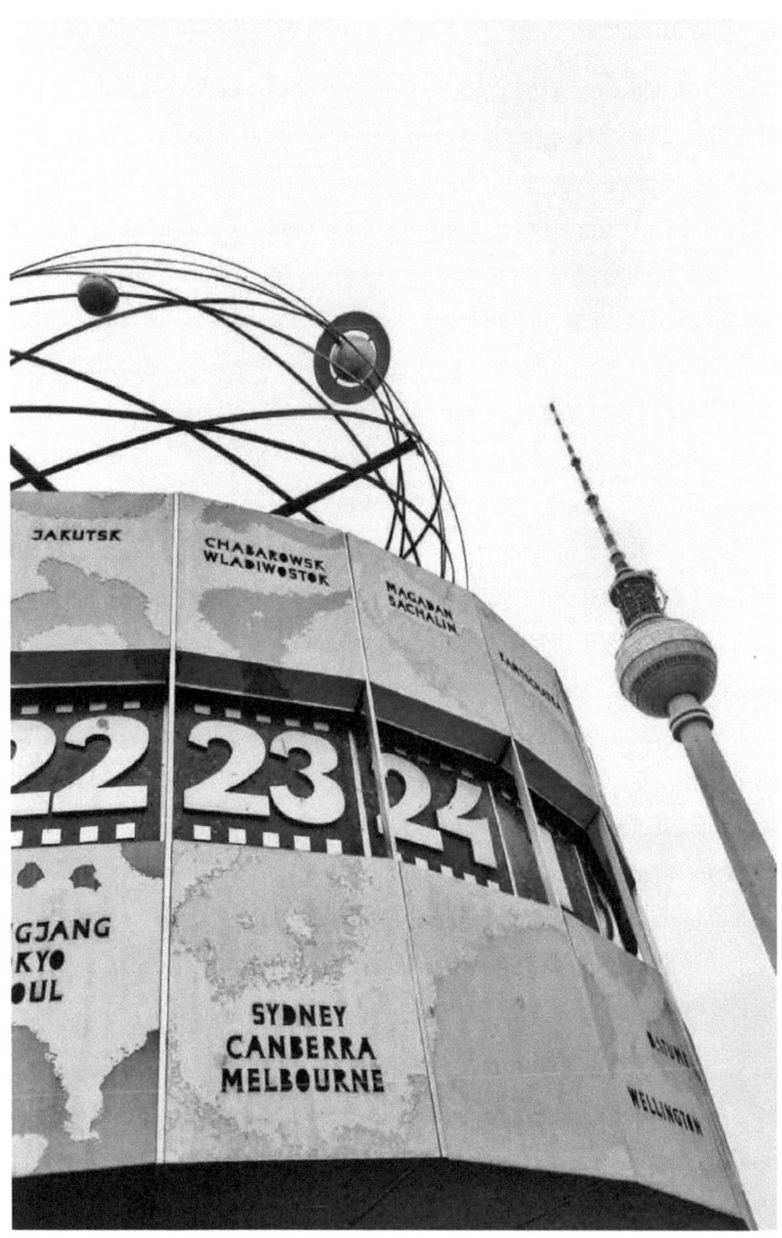

Weltzeituhr (the world time clock), Alexanderplatz, Berlin. Photo by Christiane Wagner, 2015.

4. Urban reconfigurations

With regard to the reproduction of the productive forces - the object of work, the means of production with their technologies and their workforce - we can say that the *sine qua non* condition is not only the reproduction of their "qualification", but also the reproduction of dependence on a system, of submission to the dominant ideology in a *strict* way or through the realization of the elements in communication by the ideological practices that exist in the institutions. In the day-to-day practice of communication, it is necessary for the image to be represented as an important element so that each idea is perceived as a power, capable of launching an approach towards economic development objectives. In other words, for Althusser, the institutions represent, in each of the ideological apparatuses of the state, what the system is. For each of them, there are different institutions and organizations that constitute it and form a system that is the way the infrastructure works, in which each apparatus (institutions, organizations, foundations, clubs, communities, groups, associations, parties, for-profit or not-for-profit entities, etc) is ideological. Ideologization by institutions is not only made up of ideas, it is also necessary to materialize them, in other words, to organize them, to subject them to action, in order to make them a reality. For ideology to exist, there must be the means to materialize it and the means, on the other hand, are not ideology, but reality. In the field of aesthetics, we find the realization of ideologies in the current themes of the cultural context. In fact, the observations allow us to classify the theory under the bourgeois IEA (Ideological State Apparatus) and its theoretical and applied usefulness in art and politics.

We use as an example the art event in Sao Paulo, from September 25 to December 12, 2010, the *29^e^ Bienal de Săo Paulo,* whose theme *was Art and Politics.* The implementation of the theme by many artists around the world was an ideological achievement to express their views on the political context of their countries and the world. We can often find works that are controversial as well as naive. In order to affirm this ideological representation, we say, according to analyses of the IEA, that it is an element of reproduction of its submission to the rules of order established by the dominant ideology. The art at the event in question proposes the theme of *Art and Politics* from the point of view of an ideological institution of the capitalist bourgeois IEA, a place where art is entirely the essential medium of the IEAs that correspond, with which the bourgeois class, through art as the medium of the apparatus, competently represents its ideology. This must be real, but before this can be achieved, there are intelligent and possible maneuvers in the system of the bourgeois class, which is able to articulate social movements by making them believe that they are active subjects, when they are part of the system, passive subjects. Brecht perceived these maneuvers when he was influenced by the work of Karl Marx (*das Kapital)* in his epic theater plays. His main audience was the proletariat and the trade union, and Brecht sought to break all illusions by distancing himself.

The sense of illusion is typical of the system's maneuvers, in which there are many ideologies looking for their conditions to be realized under the effects of the class struggle and, above all, under the ideology of the state, which is the power of the ruling class. The actions for integration, which lead the capitalist regime towards bourgeois ideology, are political maneuvers subject to the rules of state ideology. According to Louis Althusser[31] , it is the ideology of the bourgeois state that dominates the political system. The bourgeoisie has at its disposal a whole series of techniques established to deal with the risks in certain circumstances, those of difficulties or of functioning. With regard to the imaginary, in order to approach the contemporary image in the current world market system, it is necessary to review the scheme of structures and infrastructures of the state, according to Althusser's analyses, in order to organize ideas around consumer society, that is, to obtain a starting point so that we can situate ourselves in the system of ideas referring to life in society, in the world of images, through the eyes of aesthetics in its journey to contemporaneity. Firstly, the questions: is artistic realization in contemporary times in a situation of interdependence with social structures and relationships? What is the freedom of expression in the arts? What personal or collective experiences have space through the arts in contemporary society?

31 ALTHUSSER, Louis. *On reproduction*. Paris : PUF, 1995.

In order to understand the context of the arts and ideological dynamics, we can use a theory that is external to the superstructure in relation to the infrastructure, according to the mode of production that globalized and contemporary society exercises, analyzing technology and science as ideology, through the work of Jürgen Habermas .[32]

Understanding society and also the nature of actions is part of the complexity of knowledge throughout the development of technique, the art of creating and producing. We seek to understand the important concepts and contexts in which artistic or technical production has played a role. We base ourselves, in general terms, on ancient Greece and the socio-historical course of the West in the world of artistic production.

Thus, in a chronology of ruptures, retakes of values, movements, wars, revolutions and innovations, which have always led man to the pursuit of pleasure, freedom, imagining "happiness" and believing in the existence of a "truth" and, above all, that it is good. However, without judging values, when analyzing the structures of society and its dynamics of functioning, organizing and restructuring all the elements, and all the possibilities of relationships between them, even from the point of view of a repressive apparatus, it has been verified, above all, that the vast majority of discussions and analyses are guided by the theories of Karl Marx. But to understand all the interpretations is, above all, to understand and accept that new interpretations are still possible, and that the world is not different, but the same, in its constant evolution. The year 1968 was very significant for those young students and Marxists who sought to reverse the system, relying on theories that understood the state as a repressive apparatus. The theories of Marcuse, the structuralist thinking of Altusser, or even the leadership of Jean Paul Sartre with his work and editions of *Modern Times* sustained the rebellion of the students at that time and they especially believed in communism. Today, however, we see a different reality, with reports, for example, of Charles de Gaulle's agreement with the workers and, of course, a clarification of the way of understanding capital (*das Kapital),* without the commitment to the social context that

32 HABERMAS, Jürgen. *Technik und Wissenschaft als "Ideologie".* Frankfurt: Suhrkamp, 1968.

the intellectuals of that period lived, and even more so, experiencing, in 1989, the end of the Cold War, with the fall of the Berlin Wall. This event confirmed for almost the entire world, with the exception of North Korea, that communism in practice through Marxism had not taken hold as an ideology and, until recently, also with Cuba. In view of these elements, among others, there has been enough time for new thinkers, born or still children in the 1960s and 1970s, to understand the consequences of this era, that is, of a new generation. Children of *Woodstock* or *Peace and Love*, who even though they admired the "Age of Aquarius" or the rock classics, grew up in shopping malls or under narratives of adventures and space discoveries. A generation that is part of the technological development with films and literature that aroused interest in scientific discoveries and high technology; but still, on the other hand, living with a minority that keeps the ideas of that time alive. Such as, for example, the music and films and themes of the *nouvelle vague*, which were important on the French political scene in the 1970s, but which today, in the perception of this current generation, under the effects of high-tech cinema, are no more than films representative of a context, of a past history. Other great cinematic achievements are also considered in this scenario, of course under the influence of the film industry. With the Cold War, the world read and saw not only the narratives about incredible secret missions and all the highly efficient and "secret" technology as fiction, but in fact saw and read them as reality, since the first computers reached their best performance on the market, after being used by the state for defense strategies. This scenario influenced the children of a large majority who represented the counterculture of 1968 and who became a very important generation for the greatest of all revolutions in the 1980s: the Technological Revolution. There was also a strong commitment to what is known as sustainable development. And more recently, in 2011, a highly technological and deterritorialized youth won democracy, using the new technologies in their convergence through social networks, making the biggest breakthrough of recent times. Young people have achieved what could not have been imagined, a revolution in search of democracy in the Arab world, and indeed they have. It now remains to be seen, in another stage, how the organization and control of these countries, which have been going through a period of transition and chaos for six years, will be handled. It is precisely from this point that we will situate ourselves, in the great importance of these revolutions, so that today we can reflect abstracted from interpretations of capital *(das Kapital)* and, consequently, a Marxism that has not proved so efficient in practice. In order to understand the need for rational control by technology or science, in response to Marcuse's thinking[33] , Habermas situates us in the consequence of what rationality consists of, according to Max Weber[34] , in the choices of strategies, the use of technologies and the organization of systems in an appropriate way according to the objectives and conditions imposed. In this way, we consider the need for actions that have control over the system, nature or society, in other words, the way in which control can be achieved. This doesn't mean that such control is exercised as politics, but that it contains politics. It is thus understood that the meaning of a policy is intrinsic to the existence of the individual in society, in its public space *(polis),* as a citizen *(politicus)*.

With the great technological transformations, with the transition to a new era, not the "aquarium" era, but the digital one. The whole relationship established between productive forces, which have increased and become institutionalized with this technological and scientific progress, has gone beyond the proportions known to theorists who believed in the existence of a repressive apparatus, a system that produced both constructive and destructive social work in an articulated way in diffuse divisions, which conditioned individuals to submission.

This discontent would lead to a revolution, even if the individuals all felt powerless under a repressive force. But even so, what are the limits of freedom of expression? Liberal democracy has made the technological revolution possible, with the advent of globalization and the Internet, which has enabled communication without borders, even if control still remains. In part, through Habermas' responses to Herbert Marcuse's analysis in his work entitled *Technics and Science as "Ideology"*[35] , we can think of pertinent answers to the most important questions regarding interdependence in the

33 HABERMAS, J. *Antworten auf Herbert Marcuse*. Frankfurt am Main, Suhrkamp, 1968.
34 WEBER, Max. *Kultur und Gesellschaft, Industrializirung und Kapitalismus.* Vol. II Frankfurt am Main, 1965.
35 HABERMAS, Jürgen. *Technik und Wissenschaft als "Ideologie".* Frankfurt : Suhrkamp, 1968. *Id. La technique et la science comme "idéologie".* Paris: Gallimard, 1973, for the French translation. Jean-René Ladmiral.

relations of the contemporary system. For this thinker, there is a paradox in the thought that there might be repression, as Marcuse previously believed, stating that repression would disappear from the population's consciousness because the legitimization of domination brings about a new situation as a consequence of the advantages of this domination of nature and production, which is always to offer better benefits. We can therefore see in practice that many people who defended communism became, for example, great advertisers in the 1980s, or even famous artists who knew how to work their own image in front of their own art, following the logic of consumer society and benefiting from this system. In this way, the existing relations of production are presented as technically necessary forms of organization in a rationalized society. The rationality clarified by Habermas shows the ambiguity of Max Weber's meaning: on the one hand, it presents itself as discontent as a critical calculation of the development of the productive forces, which allow meaningless repression to be dismantled, and which belonged to historically outdated production relations. On the other hand, as calculations to justify production relations as an institutional *status*, in line with real objectives. In short, Habermas shows something that Marcuse couldn't have known, which is the consequences of an arbitrary scientific and technological development that has reached a configuration in which the productive forces experience new relations with the relations of production. Marcuse's writings date from the 1950s and 1960s in particular. Now, in contemporary times, we are not looking for demystification, political enlightenment (*Aufklărung*), but legitimization. It is understood that there is a collusion between the state and society, in order to take advantage of the benefits that all this development in technology and science offers. If, on the one hand, the force of the state's power to control is exercised, on the other, resistance and the search for the rights of freedom are concentrated as a force of the masses. Therefore, two opposing forces, equally capable of maintaining a point by neutralizing the differences, in other words, a system balanced by its own conditions of survival. In addition to Habermas' analysis of Marcuse's situation, there are a number of events, reproducing the words used by the author, which are confirmed when we consider the theme addressed in the previous chapter, about ecology, sustainable development and fair trade, which would be "legitimizing" a new economic policy with targets set for 2050 by the UN conventions (Kyoto, Durban and COP 21 in Paris), emphasizing the *long term.* A rationalized emphasis which, in Weber's sense, is a rationalization of social structures, also becoming the real motive in the Freudian sense, to maintain an objectively outdated and concealed domination, by means of references that serve the fundamental interests of the state and the community.

To this end, rationality is itself science and technique, organizing the elements and offering progress, a simple sense of productive power. A sense of development that, due to the consequences of capitalism, has been stigmatized by being understood as a form of manipulation, as intentional domination.

If the theories themselves are ambiguous about this supposed rationality as dominance by technology and science, this proves that any intelligent reflection would cast doubt on this condition. To confirm this thought, all we have to do is check, throughout the history of mankind, that inventions have almost always had no purpose in their origin, or when they have, it hasn't been for evil, but for good. We always see evil as a consequence of use, or in other words, misuse; it is society that corrupts man. But in general, it is human nature, in Rousseau's sense, that gives man the only natural passions, which are love of self, love of neighbor and the desire to preserve good and peace. Perhaps for the reasons mentioned above, the desire to preserve good and peace, the aesthetic experience, that is, the feeling of beauty - of the good and the beautiful - of some works has been consecrated by time and has made them masterpieces. Regardless of the criteria used by experts to judge the aesthetics of works that have made up the history of Western art, but because of the values of their eternal presence, undergoing cultural transformations. Works that pass through time and continue to be contemplated, touching the sensibilities of their observers, a public that is not specialized in art, but that perceives in the image values intrinsic to its human nature, which is the feeling of beauty, with the need for an understanding (*Verstand*), in the Kantian sense, by which it is possible to understand an art object, understanding it through the senses. Remember that the experience of transcendental aesthetics has the meaning of perception *(perzeption*). Let's take it again: through the meaning that the object offers - if the work of art has the power to reach the senses - if it is perceived, then one can think about the art object and understand it according to each individual's repertoire and then conceptualize it. The concept (*Begriffe*) and perception offer the individual sensations (*Empfindung*) that influence their senses (*Sinnlichkeit*) and, finally, make it possible to awaken their interests or desires (*Erscheinung*) for the work of art. If, on the one hand, we are concerned with what exists in the world (*Seiendes*) through empiricism, on the other, we are always questioning and looking for answers that we can't find. We only find different forms of answers to the same things in different configurations. If these answers are resolving or solving things in the world, then it means constant reconfiguration.

However, given the complex relationship between the phenomena of human existence (*Sein*) and a sense of innovation, we look to Western tradition to think about "innovation" in the face of so many configuring elements that we find in space. We're not going to mention a specific space for contemplating a work, such as a museum or gallery, but rather public space. This is a space that presents all aspects of everyday life and which, throughout the history of artistic creations, since antiquity, and where, even with the transformation of perception, any individual, initiated or not in the arts, could have feelings for art and be moved. Whether it's the frescoes in the Sistine Chapel designed by Michelangelo, especially when you see the *Last Judgement*, or the contemporary values present in the United Nations Headquarters building in New York, in front of War and Peace, by Cândido Portinari.

In its history, art has transformed the way we understand it. It doesn't matter which metropolis it is, we can be sure that technical evolution and the importance of scientific status have contributed to elevating art and its counterparts to great importance. However, in the same proportion, trivialization under subjective value judgments, based on taste in its popular aspects in relation to the polysemy of meaning is, above all, in the face of an immense diversity of values, the orientation of artistic speculation. The transformation of ways of life, from prehistoric times to the life of contemporary society, offers us an immense inventory of all the achievements that would not have space to be presented here. Therefore, in general terms, what represents the configuration of a contemporary image, in its search for innovation, is to understand that the dynamics of global metropolises, in their process of transformation, always seek to meet the needs of the *modus vivendi.* Not just by the means already mentioned, which in isolation would lead to other reflections on constant artistic movements, changes in the system and market, production and work relations, new objects and services; everything, in short, as a consequence of globalization and standardization in the configuration of a single image. This image is the representation of a standard civilization. Art finds itself in the face of technological and scientific developments, in a scenario of contemporary universality that is not only about social transformations, but above all about the environment. We can confirm this situation by studying Pierre Francastel's work, *Art and Technique*[36] , and with his words consolidate it as a consequence of technical evolution:

"Désormais les objectes où l'activité de l'homme pénètrent uniformément dans toutes les régions de la terre ; et leur grau toujours plus grand d'accessibilité réduit les distinctions anciennes de classes. The result for art, insofar as it participates in the material transformation of the world, is a force of pénétration at the same time as the abandonment of one of the most striking aspects of its ancient activity. Il ne souligne plus, desormais, la specificité de formes réservées à certaines categories étroites de personnes - potentats ou initiés - il exalte au contraire la généralité des perceptions et des messages." [37]

In the first part[38] , we commented on the aspects of art as a tribal experience, for the purpose of sharing it today with cultures constituted as a historical community. In addition to the fact that this primitive coexistence with the contemporary coexistence of ethnic groups or ethnic minorities in relation to the civilization of the global metropolis. As early as the 1950s and 1960s, according to Francastel's observations,

---

36 FRANCASTEL, Pierre. *Art et technique, aux XIXe et XXe siècles*. France: Minuit, 1956.

37 "Now the objects that represent man's activity penetrate uniformly into all regions of the earth, and their ever-increasing degree of accessibility reduces the differences of previous classes. The result in art, as it participates in the material transformation of the world, is a growing force of infiltration, at the same time as the abandonment of any of the most striking aspects of its previous activity. It no longer emphasizes the peculiar forms reserved for certain categories of close people - powerful or initiated - but rather exalts the generality of perceptions and messages." (Cit. translated from the French by Christiane Wagner). *Ibid*., 1956, p. 224.

38 Cf. p. 32.

the manifestations of certain folkloric or popular art groups in the face of realizations, observed by this theorist as currents that offer no resistance to realizations in the field of the arts, with characteristics identical to primitive objects and images. However, at the same time as a standardization has taken place in the metropolises since the end of the Second World War and especially today, in the 21st century, some subtleties remain regarding the regional transformations of some cities in relation to the search for new values.

Even so, as a *modus vivendi*, we can see strong differentiating marks between cultures and tastes. For example, the Brazilian carnival, which is very strong in Rio de Janeiro, Bahia, Sao Paulo, Recife and other regions of Brazil, with the exception of the south. Or, for example, the Maori culture in New Zealand. So, in the words[39] of the sociologist Waldenyr Caldas, despite a global trend towards standardization, the appeal of the cultural industry and everything in it as a product to be marketed, it would be almost impossible for the Maori to dance samba, nor would carnival take over the days of the week and the streets in New Zealand. Nor would the majority of people in Rio de Janeiro have their faces tattooed all their lives. This sociologist from the University of São Paulo, who studies the theories of the Frankfurt School, says that in his analysis of the theory of the Cultural Industry, Adorno mainly questions the quality of the artistic work, aesthetics, and discusses taste and ideology; he is even less optimistic when he considers that the Cultural Industry has a deliberate dynamic of integration from a dominant consumer class; which, according to Caldas' observations, consists of a dynamic of integration in appearance only. Caldas confirms:

"It cannot be realized because, among other things, it violates the principle of social stratification in capitalism. In this sense, it is a utopia. At the same time, the attempt to make high art (which can be understood as erudite art) and low art (popular art) a product accessible to the whole of society would be to the detriment of both."[40]

So, even if we can consume in the same way in Paris, Berlin and Sao Paulo, even if the

39 CALDAS, Waldenyr. *A cultura lùdica brasileira* [electronic message] Personal information. Received by : Christiane WAGNER, on 14/06/2012.
40 *Id. Utopia of taste*. Sao Paulo: Brasiliense, 2009, p. 121.

configuration of the image by the arts and their counterparts is standardized, the differences are subtle and thc characteristics of each culture remain resistant to hegemony. Popular art, with its characteristics still of distant and primitive origins, would lose its function of realizing and expressing the values of each culture or community as an essential element of existence. However, it remains to be seen, in the face of the transformations that industrial evolution presents, what remains as a non-industrial characteristic.

The studies of the theories of the so-called Frankfurt School were of great importance for the moment that Germany was experiencing, in the face of the political and social conditions of a post-World War II industrial scenario, but above all, due to the inheritance of classic Western philosophical thought, influenced by Kant, Hegel and Marx, which marked the development of the 20th century through two major wars, ideological differences between capitalism and communism, and the great revolutions and movements of modernity, with regard to the development of industry and cultural production. The theories that represented this line of research had as their precursors the philosophers of the *Goethe-Universităt Frankfurt am Main* (Goethe University, located in Frankurt, on the banks of the river Main). They are: Max Horkheimer and Theodor Adorno who, while developing a work published in 1947 entitled *The Dialectic of Reason* (*Dialektik der Aufklărung*), coined the term *Cultural Industry* (*Kulturindustrie*). The term was intended to differentiate popular culture from mass culture. Apparently, these terms could lead to confusion, because the popular, inherent to the people, cannot be the same as a standardized majority - the mass. The aims of this line of study were to analyze industrial development as culture.

Firstly, in Germany, and then in America, due to the political exile of these theorists, who left Germany for the United States. With their new experiences in a market culture with great potential, these theorists focused their studies on the industrial production of cultural goods and the effects it had on society.

The consequences of industrial production led society towards a new reality in which traditional culture was changing rapidly. All values, especially aesthetic ones, were changing. The most important aspect discussed by the Frankfurt School thinkers was the production relationship, which prioritized quantity over quality. They perceived an ideological dynamic towards a standardized culture, with economic objectives aimed at profit. According to Adorno, this would make the quality of an artistic work, especially musical and literary works, impossible. With mass production, individuals would be intensely consuming "cultural products" in terms of quantity, responding to a dynamic of constant new demands and the speed of productivity, hindering not only the quality of the production, but also of the work, which would result in a disqualified product compared to the erudite work, due to the lack of time needed to deepen an understanding of the work or even to produce it. They therefore saw this dynamic as a way of manipulating the market system.

In addition to their precursors, Horkheimer and Adorno, these theories have the importance of the analyses of Hebert Marcuse and, in a more differentiated way, those of Walter Benjamin. These works were partially published in Germany and the United States, and it was only in the mid-1970s that they began to take on greater importance. In France, they only began to arouse interest in French thought in the 1980s, as Marc Jimenez, a connoisseur of the Frankfurt School, who also translated Adorno's *Aesthetic Theory* and interpreted most of the School's theories into French in philosophy and the sciences of art, tells us. This French philosopher and Germanist from the Sorbonne also explains that Horkheimer and Adorno realized that the administrators of a democratic or democratized culture were in fact obeying the imperatives of the market, benefiting from the dissemination of the myths of a traditional bourgeois culture, which they called the "mystification of the masses". With this in mind, not only Adorno, but also Marcuse, developed their aesthetic theories. For Adorno in particular, he defended modern art, as long as it could be of the highest quality due to the new techniques, even offering a certain hermeticism as a form of reaction to the manipulation of needs in the system, in which the power was that of technique or of those who dominated society economically. With Marcuse, guided by Martin Heidegger with the thesis *Hegel's Ontology and the foundation of a theory of historicity,* 1932 (*L'ontologie de Hegel et le fondement d'une théorie de l'historicité*), with a great influence from Heidegger, in the work *Being and Time*, 1927 (*L'être et le temps*), this thinker develops a phenomenological reasoning due to the writings of Wilhelm Dilthey (1833-1911). Dilthey[41] was very significant, especially at the end of his scientific output through the values that founded the social sciences and contributed to studies in aesthetics, because of the way he understood the world of the arts, knowing very well the course of artistic achievement in Germany and Italy, and recognizing that artistic activity was rooted in the totality of human actions. Marcuse thus laid the foundations for his concrete philosophy. However, even with the prospect of delving deeper into research alongside Heidegger, with the arrival of Nazism, Marcuse parted company with Heidegger and joined the Frankfurt School theorists.

For French thought, even if the articles that represent the influence of Frankfurt School thought were not yet important, there are records that in 1936, in Paris, Marcuse and Adorno published in collaboration *Studies on Authority* and *the Family* and, consecutively, articles and works were developed and their way of thinking evolved and met with the materialist thinking common to Horkheimer and Adorno. However, by bringing Marx's theories closer to Freud's, he promoted not only a rapprochement between psychoanalysis and Marxism, but also a critique of bourgeois ideology and a political practice that encouraged young people to rebel against capitalist authority and adhere to a more liberal approach to sexuality. Marcuse evolves his thinking until he arrives at theories that analyze capitalist society in a negative way, dealing with aspects of repression and the reality of consumer society, affirming that pleasure is not a cultural value, but only discussing the irrational aspects of an industrial society, especially in the relationship between desires and needs that guides industrial production, or even the conflicts between desire and lack. Specifically with regard to technological development, Marcuse hoped for an equivalent freedom for man, in

41 A configuration (*eine Gestaltung*) which defines the artistic activity of form and the work of art, is found by Dilthey in a common place. Starting from Kant's conclusions, Wilhem Dilthey studies the constitution of being as having a meaning through its historical knowledge, in which understanding is not in instrojection, but always through history. He develops a line of reasoning, seeking to distinguish between the natural sciences and the sciences of the spirit. He shows that both are justified, concluding that we clarify nature, but it is through intimate experience (*das Seelenleben*) that we understand it, i.e. by experiencing, expressing and understanding. Dilthey is considered the founder of the human sciences (*die Geisteswissenschaften*). EHRICH, Florian. *Der Vater der Geisteswissenschaften*. Available at: <www.dradio.de/dkultur/>.
Accessed on: 01/10/2011.

relation to necessity as well as the sacrifice of energy and time. But still focusing his analysis on political aspects, he developed an aesthetic focused on everyday life through politics, looking for meanings in the work of art in modernity, characterized as a form of protest against the system. The importance of Brecht's works during modernity has great significance as an artistic achievement that breaks with the classical forms of the arts, and Marcuse also exemplifies this quality of subversive work to the system with Brecht's *Mãe Coragem*. But above all, his thinking was marked by the expression "affirmative culture", due to his article entitled *On the Affirmative Character of Culture*, 1937. In industrial society, modern, democratic culture was developed by the dynamics of mass consumption of cultural goods, renouncing the forms offered by the art of antiquity, which were the means of transferring the fulfillment of desires through art. In psychoanalysis, this process is called sublimation. Instead of finding ways to sublimate desires through art, in modern society, pleasure is found through material and concrete resources, a material culture, which is the opposite of an idealistic culture and is therefore less affirmative, thus characterizing modern culture, which does not create mechanisms to progressively transform reality. This is discussed in detail in the first chapters about Brecht's *catharsis* and epic theater, which sought to break away from illusion and bring the audience closer to social reality. Still in this period, without enough time for the political and social transformations to take the necessary course for new ways of interpreting the system in its development to emerge, these theories were intensely discussed and valued in Latin America, specifically in Brazil. In 1964, with the advent of the coup d'état, Brazil began to live under military authoritarianism that lasted until 1985. An extremely anti-democratic and repressive scenario, in which the military forces exercised their power. The theories of Adorno and Marcuse responded to the reality of this period and supported the first research in sociology and studies in communication and culture, by a few intellectuals and, above all, those resistant to this manipulation by the state. In 1969, at the Faculty of Philosophy of the University of São Paulo, located in Rua Maria Antônia, Professor Gabriel Cohn introduced the[42] texts he had translated from German

42 COHN, Gabriel. *Communication and the cultural industry.* São Paulo: Companhia Editora Nacional/EDUSP, 1971.

into Portuguese and influenced a whole generation that has since become disciples of the Frankfurt School. This included names like Ciro Marcondes, Gilberto Vaconcellos and Olgaria Matos, professors in communication sciences, sociology and philosophy. As well as the sociologist Waldenyr Caldas, who had Gabriel Cohn as his advisor throughout his training at the Faculty of Philosophy and Social Sciences at the University of São Paulo, representing not only that period, but also the evolution of thought from that time onwards. As well as representative works for the Brazilian scene at the time, based on Adorno's theories, Brazilian popular music, mass literature, in short, the consumer and communication society, this thinker presents, above all, the Brazilian political and social reality in contemporary times, obviously in Sao Paulo, as a metropolis and the result of social and cultural transformations.

On the international scene, according to Jimenez's current lessons, the uncompromising and negative positions in Adorno's criticism are hardly acceptable today. But he clarifies that Adorno, even before his death in 1969, had understood that his theory of modernity was confronting the decline of modern art, *kitsch* was taking more space in the face of the well-established power of the cultural industry, subject to market profits. Thus, today the expression "cultural industries" prevails, designating the new technologies with the aim of producing, disseminating and practicing art and culture. But even so, this does not prevent Adorno and Horkheimer from realizing the risk of a standardized and globalized technoculture to the detriment of individual, differentiated and original experiences, says Marc Jimenez.

But in another way, not through sociological and philosophical aspects, but through semantics itself, when we analyze forms, regardless of materials, but mainly through language, we see the results that imagination presents in a timeless way. Pierre Francastel cited, in the chapter *Fonction de l'art dans la societé mécanisée* (Function of art in a mechanized society), that modern art, often imaginative, by presenting time and space in an abstract way, participates in the daily lives of individuals both through purely figurative signs and manufactured objects. We understand, therefore, that even before language evolves, reaches writing and achieves an almost perfect communication capacity, if we consider the differences in intelligence, knowledge and mastery by the population and, above all, the different languages, the pictorial language still continues to unify the communication of different cultures, accompanying the new forms of representation. Because new technologies offer new possibilities, regardless of any resemblance by the image to the characteristics of a specific art from any time or place.

Still, under the effects of modernity, Francastel places us in an evolution through a temporal example of the rhythm of life that represented French society, with a difference of a century when he mentions that Victor Hugo, in 1850, said that the world would go by wagon and speak French, and that, in 1950, the author himself said in his work[43] that the world would go by plane and would draw and sculpt as in Paris. Today, however, we would say that the world has become de-territorialized and we no longer find time or even place, and Morin asks: where is the world going? Apparently, the contemporary image is configured in its visual narratives. From the first major works in the *polis*, and still marking references to Paris. Let's take a look at the information in *Art and Technique :*[44]

"It was with Toulouse-Lautrec, in particular, that we went from a form of advertising through design to a purely visual form. When Cesar Birotteau wanted to touch the Parisian public in 1840, Balzac told us about the shop window he decorated in the center of Paris. It is a written advertisement. The letters placed on the glaze of a shop window highlight the merits of La Reine des Crèmes, in a context directly related to the famous collections of La Mésangère, which was the target of the Directoire or Restauration movement. Daumier's style, just as much as Gavarni's or Devéria's, implies legend. Throughout the 19th century, the image illustrated or materialized a proposition. Then, on the other hand, the legend recedes, fires. The image speaks all by itself; it is enriched no longer by a design but by a color. La réclame participates ainsi au développement le plus ésotérique de l'art de ce temps."[45]

---

43 FRANCASTEL, Pierre. *Art and technique in the 19th and 20th centuries*. Paris : Gallimard, 1956, p. 225.
44 *Ibid., Op. Cit.* p. 225.
45 *It is with Toulouse-Lautrec, in particular, that we move from a form of advertising by the system to a purely visual form. When Cesar Birotteau wanted to touch the Parisian public in 1840, Balsac described the shop window he decorated in the center of Paris. It was a written advertisement. The letters on the glass of the window sold the merits of the Queen of Creams, in a painting directly taken from the famous collections of La Mésangère, a late echo of the taste of the Administration or the Restoration. Daumier's style, as much as Gavarni's or Devéria's, involved the caption. Throughout*

Drawing became technically reproducible through woodcutting and this - the technique responsible for the reproduction of writing - led to the printing press. Reproduction began with the first technique, woodcut, followed by copperplate printing, etching and lithography. Through these techniques, the graphic arts began to illustrate everyday life. At the end of the 19th century, with the advent of photography, the process of reproducing images was put on the same level as the spoken word.

Another important literary work for the universe of images is Marcel Proust's novel, *À la recherche du temps perdue*[46] . In it, we find, in addition to the city, the Parisian society of his time. It is a written work, but because of its narrative style, it is visually configured. The process of technical reproduction of the narrative develops in the story with great intensity. Without forgetting that urban concentration is reinforced by the industrial revolution and, concomitantly, the reproduction and distribution of images is emphasized. What differs throughout history are the techniques and means of reproduction. As well as the purpose of reproduction and the accounts of these images represented in stories and communication. Images are of great importance. The reader develops their imagination, developing fantasy and reality by interpreting a way of seeing the context. Visual poetic boundaries also allow free access to the imagination. The story transports the reader to the values that can lead to illusion, conditioning the sequence of images for the emotional. It is precisely this work by Proust that Walter Benjamin, together with Franz Hessel, worked on translating into German at the beginning of the 20th century.

A major influence on Benjamin's knowledge, like other literary figures such as Baudelaire and Balzac, who have also been translated or commented on. Benjamin searched for meaning, for knowledge in the world of objects, using inductive research methods in his own way, valuing the meaning of empiricism rather than that of a Western tradition that has always sought an essence beyond the material universe. Thus, in an era that was experimenting with the novelties that the industrial revolution

---

the 19th century, the image illustrated or materialized a purpose. Today, on the contrary, the caption is receding, disappearing. The image speaks for itself; it is enriched not only by value but by color. Advertising thus participates in the most esoteric artistic development of these times.

46 PROUST, Marcel. *À la recherche du temps perdu*. Paris : Gallimard, 1999.

was promoting, and in which a vast experience was allowed with all forms of object presentation, production and development and, of course, a fertile scenario for creations, interpretations and discussions, this was modernity. In Paris, especially in the artistic world, aesthetics and morality were intensely debated. The object, the star of the stage, was a reason to challenge bourgeois canons and tradition. The iconoclasts emerged with Dadaism, inciting disorganization and secularization in the artistic world in Zurich, and quickly taking over the scene in Berlin, Paris and other European cities. Apart from all the incessant descriptions of the Dadaist manifestations, let's see that, in fact, all the anti-aesthetic manifestations sought to offer a new way of looking at objects, in other words, the act of creating, destroying in order to rebuild. Numerous artistic forms emerged from reconfigurations in the universe of letters and images, even finally being called an "aesthetic carnival" by Marcel Duchamp, who himself believed that this was the way to discover the "magic of the work of art". What a paradox! With iconoclastic principles, the Dadaists proclaimed the iconolatry of a new form of image, consecrating their forms of artistic creation. The biggest star of this period, Duchamp's *ready-made*, established the object - of lesser aesthetic importance, but with great notoriety in everyday life, for example, the urinal and the bicycle wheel - as a work of art, offering the observer a change in the perception of known values and, from then on, in an unprecedented way, offering new possibilities in the "space" for perception. It was a way of perceiving things, of changing artistic values, and one that still resists today in contemporary art as an antidote to the purists and conservatives who valued the aesthetics prevalent in the 17th and 18th centuries.

In short, a milestone to situate us in this constant search for new forms of realization by many and also by many others who seek to understand the meaning of the world through things. And, of course, even though it was short and remarkable, Dadaism opened up the frontiers of creativity and imagination in the world of the arts for the advent of Surrealism, which sought other ways of understanding the relationship between human beings and their material world. However, without "destroying" this material conception of the world, it absented itself from its apparent reality, taking refuge in the psychoanalytic universe of dreams and delirium. Paris, capital of great events, is a source of seduction for all those interested in the achievements of the human being.

Walter Benjamin sought to understand the world through everyday life and theoretical discussions. The influence that this scenario exerted at the beginning of the 20th century, with the company of Brecht, Aragon, Breton, Franz Hessel, or even his religious beliefs, experience with drugs, childhood memories, or even the balanced orientations of Theodor Adorno, enabled Benjamin to reflect on what resulted in a vast and, above all, fragmented oeuvre. Walter Benjamin is an important reference point for much of the most important research into the image because his work portrays the "disintegration of culture into goods that can be possessed by humanity", as Jürgen Habermas confirms,[47] . *He goes* on to say that, publicly, Benjamin never spoke of a revocation of culture (*Aufhebung der Kultur*)[48] . We can see the importance of Benjamin's work in relation to the image in his journey through the city of Paris, through the records we find published today of his way of observing the transformations involved in the techniques of mass seduction and all aspects of human fulfillment. With his work *"Le livre de passages[49] "* (the book of passages), in which he describes the years from 1927 to 1929, and resumes in 1934, we see the main features of an image of the 19th century capital, through the universal exhibitions, fashion, advertising, stores, passageways, iron and glass buildings, the streets of Paris, and more: Parisian life. But, above all, a very important aspect: the definition of his concept, in 1935, of the "aura" that arises from his analysis of the forms of reproduction and this relationship with the effects of images on society. Taking as a starting point an image in its intention as art, and art throughout its history, showing its existence and presence through the copy, but maintaining its characteristics of an origin of time and place through the "aura". In other words, it is not the original, nor is it the aesthetic experience of the moment and space in which the work was made, but only the knowledge of it.

---

47 *"des Zerfalls der Kultur in Güter, die der Menschheit ein Objekt des Besitzes werden konnen".* HABERMAS, Jürgen. *Politik, Kunst, Religion.* Stuttgart: Reclam, 1978, p. 50.

48 *Ibid., Op. Cit.,* p. 50.

49 BENJAMIN, Walter. *Paris, capitale du XIXe siècle - le livre des passages.* Paris: Les éditions du CERF, 2009.

Works of art have always been reproducible, and the process of technical reproduction has developed with great intensity throughout history. What has differed are the techniques and means of reproduction. As well as the purpose of the reproductions and the relationship of these images as expression, representation, narrative or communication.

One of the most important early works in the history of narrative reproduction is Trajan's Column. Not in the sense of a copy of the original, but as the image of a story reproduced and transmitted. The narrative carved on the Column, the conquest of Emperor Trajan, was reproduced by the architectural work representing power with striking and victorious scenes from the Roman Empire. To this day, in Rome, this feat symbolizes a tradition, as well as being a striking example of the importance of the image in the construction of the social imagination, the rhythm of life of a great Western civilization. At that time, the importance of the construction of the emperor's image and its reproduction were worked out according to the technical possibilities that had been achieved and developed.

At the time, the skills of the first arts still prevailed: architecture and sculpture. There were two processes for reproducing works of art: casting and minting. Only coins and terracottas were mass-produced. All other works were unique and eternal, mainly due to the state of the art, forcing eternal values to be produced. Unlike today, when the ephemeral prevails and art is reproduced on a large scale, with great perfection to be valued, in particular with advertising and cinema, where, throughout the shoot, there is the possibility of correcting scenes and, even with all the scenes ready, in editing, it is possible to select the best or even retouch. While the Greeks aimed for eternal values, such as sculpture that came from a single block, today it's different when it comes to art.

Painting, the mastery of techniques, the ability to reproduce nature and the human being, divine representation and the sense of enchantment, beauty and the sublime involved the whole of society. The reproduction of the ideal, at that time, in other times or in our time, is the image of the prevailing ideology, in all its forms of expression and technical reproduction. Technique was characterized by the mastery and knowledge of the architect, the sculptor, the artist and the craftsman. And expression, through the ability to represent ideas, is the dynamic of social relations. All evolution focuses first on achievements, on productive results and then on the consequences of the results. This process is important as a factor in social transformation, new forms of relationships and productive means.

In Walter Benjamin's essay[50] on technical reproduction, through his reflections, we understand that technical reproduction does not allow, in its moment of existence, a loss of the image of the work of art as a visual value. However, the transformations that occur with the passage of time and the relationships of ownership in relation to the original work or the distancing, these do allow the loss of the content of its authenticity. This content can be perfected through technique, but devalued because it is not the original work - Leonardo da Vinci's Mona Lisa (La Gioconda), oil on canvas; the sculpture (in marble); the *Panthéon* or the Eiffel Tower, architectures in Paris; works of art and also representative in their location and time. This authenticity means having an origin, a material state and its historical testimony to transmit a tradition. With reproduction, everything that has been transmitted by tradition disappears, because there is no testimony from the people who lived through each of these historical moments. When they lived, access to these works was selective, restricted, or they were perceived in one way or another. Some works, in their location and time, were significant for most people, as the Trajan's Column presented earlier. With it, through the moving narrative, civilization perceived the power of the Roman Emperor. The Mona Lisa (*La Gioconda*), in the Louvre; and Trajan's Column, in Rome. From the original to the reproduction, and from this to a serial reproduction, leading to the dominance of the tradition of the reproduced object. This object, reproduced by means of technology, meets the viewer in every situation, offering a current character to the continuity of the reproduction of itself, shaking up tradition and renewing culture. He became present and closer to the mass population, mainly through the cinema, without

50 BENJAMIN, Walter. *Œuvres,* Tome I, II et III. Paris: Gallimard, 2000.

considering the traditional values of cultural heritage. A phenomenon of updating time and locating works of art simultaneously in a single space and time. Human perception is not only conditioned naturally, but also historically. Nowadays, with the growing diffusion and intensity of being closer to the object, of possessing it, destroying its aura, according to the theorist Walter Benjamin, which is that which is capable of identifying a figure as unique and distant in its time and space, maintaining all the references of the original, but not its material value. The destruction of the aura is manifested in the sensory sphere as a tendency that, according to the theory, is explained by the analysis of the growing importance of a reality serving the public or the public seeking that reality. The uniqueness of the work of art is embedded in the context of tradition and is never detached from its ritual function. The earliest form of insertion of the work of art into the context of tradition was expressed in worship. The first works of art appeared at the service of a ritual, initially magical and then religious. After the emergence of photography, with technical reproducibility, the work of art was emancipated, for the first time in history, from its parasitic existence, detaching itself from ritual. As soon as the criterion of authenticity changed in the relations of artistic production, the entire social function of art was transformed. It is no longer based on ritual, but on politics.

The cult value begins to recede in the face of the exhibition value. With the first photos, without the presence of man (landscapes, views of cities and streets), the exhibition value surpasses the cult value. In these images, contemplation is free and the captions direct the viewer's reading. The controversy over artistic value in painting and photography in the 19th century became confused and unimportant, emphasizing its significance today. The reflections on the image in the public space, from the point of view of the relationship between popular art and erudite art, or the product of industrial culture, are in line with what Bejamin optimistically perceived at the beginning of the 20th century. And that, as Marc Jimenez explains when answering an important question in contemporary aesthetics, which consists of the following doubt: whether the notion of "aura", developed in the 1930s by Walter Benjamin, could today refer to the relationship between art and new technologies. There is no doubt that the new technologies can now allow images to be disseminated, transmitting works from different places and times to anyone who wants to see them. But what is more important is to understand that, despite the forms of reproduction, the original work still exists or has existed and what is transmitted is only the image - the exhibition value - as opposed to the cult value of the original. It is this value, this experience, that is understood as "aura". In contemporary times, as Jimenez explains, the meaning of this transfer of values in the face of the image is interpreted as "a decline in aura", with cultural value as political progress because it corresponds to what is now known as the "democratization of art". But there is still ambiguity, because this decline can also be interpreted as a revolution of all the functions of art, mainly the progressive end of tradition, the impoverishment of direct experiences of things in favor of immediate or mediated experiences, in the midst of the universe of reproductions, artifices and simulacra. Let's take a look at Marc Jimenez's own words about an aesthetic experience, through the new technologies, in which we find ourselves: *"mediatized proximity is real, but it can also be a darkness, a kind of opaque screen that isolates the individual and makes him alien to the reality of everyday experience.*[51] *"*

Today, with technical reproducibility, art, outside of its function in worship, apparently has no autonomy. This situation takes art in a new direction. One of its most important social functions is to create a balance between man and his environment. Man creates this balance through his representation of the environment and the representation of the world by this technology. The consequences of this technology and *mass* resources is the collective perception of the public appropriating individual modes of perception to configure the contemporary image of urban centers. The viewer's association of ideas is immediately interrupted when the image changes. The masses are responsible for any new attitude towards the image. The increase in participants led to an increase in participation. The non-committal reception that is increasingly observed in all areas of art, characterizing the profound transformations in perceptual structures, has its

51 "Media proximity is real, but it can also be an illusion, a kind of opaque screen that isolates the individual and makes them foreign to the reality of everyday experience." (excerpt translated by Christiane Wagner).
JIMENEZ, Marc. *L'esthétique contemporaine*. Paris: Klincksieck, 2004, p. 66.

privileged setting in advertising. It is in large urban centers that it is at its most original. But nothing reveals the importance of our time more clearly than the fact that the image of consumer society prevails in the very universe of the optics of what would represent a simulacrum of the urban image.

5. The global metropolis and the Brazilian image

Cultures are the presence, influence and heritage of humanity. This heritage can be universal or restricted to a small community. At the same time, a variation of culture can be considered in the dynamics of a global metropolis that keeps part of its heritage within its borders and the other, universal. Then, progressively, the subsequent complexities of development make it possible for individuals to integrate into their diverse culture, but correlative when it comes to immigration. This dynamic, through which the individual acquires a presence as a citizen, operates under the influence of achievements, transmitting tradition, education, knowledge of the language, history, art and customs. However, the diversity of cultures, whether between nations or between different nationalities concentrated in the same nation, has in its process of acculturation an intellectual, spiritual and aesthetic development. The greatest characteristic of the results is seen in the artistic practices of the present and in the works that remain in time, marking not only a cultural origin, but a process of identification and adaptations to other realities of time and space. These new realities can be understood as contemporary realizations. On the one hand, it can be the process of acculturation in a nation within its territorial limits; on the other, from the point of view of deterritorialization, of an experience through time and without a sense of space, through the digital media to new meanings, but using a reminiscence of the past.

It is not always easy to distinguish ideas of a necessary future from the historical achievements of man's intellectual, spiritual and aesthetic development. The historical presence in the sense of human self-development is also a continuous and connected process in the global metropolises. Furthermore, in the sense of progress and development of civilization, or even world civilization, the metropolis imposes a rhythm on the world under the guidelines of the hegemonic powers, through its cultural productions. Undoubtedly, by the conditions and contexts in which interpretations and "general laws of historical development" are required[52] . This is an important and interesting abstract use of arguments proposing innovations. In addition to arguments,

52 POPPER, K.R. *Apud.*, WILLIAMS, R., 2007. p. 202.

to describe the intention of new possibilities, the word "innovation" has gained importance by expressing the desire for political, economic and social changes that aim to ensure a different future for everything that was commonplace until then. However, the predominance of the term innovation has become even more common. The meaning of "common" in social history[53] in its extensive meaning ranges from what is common to a community, or as a contrast between social classes, between something that is common (*res plebeiia*) or public (*res publica*), or even as something habitual with a sense of value judgment, to refer to what is not to the taste of an elite, but of a lower social class. At the same time, to make common to many, that is, to communicate - root in the Latin action noun *Comunicationem -,* from the Latin past participle *communicare*, from *communis*, meaning "common". Also of great importance is the Latin word *communitatem*, which has the meaning of a community of relationships or feelings, and also has its origins in the word common (*communis*). In short, we are dealing with a binary relationship between community and communication that seems inseparable from each other, both in its etymological and socio-historical sense. However, any relationship with the realization of something truly innovative seems unlikely when we realize the dynamics that mark the presence and influence of cultures in large metropolises. Thus, we find in *communis* in the specific sense, what is common in the influence of human relations, of the people, in the ideals of a democracy, from the Greek *demokratia, demos* (people) *and kratos* (government). It can be said that this established general meaning of democracy has not lasted, since in its socio-political history it has had many meanings, due to the different contexts of its practices. Today, the meaning of democracy is still very ambiguous, but as far as global aspects are concerned, the broad meaning of democracy is very important in electoral and public opinion societies. Therefore, to the extent that the influence of hegemonic nations with both liberal and socialist political presences is emphasized as an integral form of the global system and worldview. Governments with ideologies that oppose each other in practice, but which, through democracy in their predominant ideals, can find a balance

53 WILLIAMS, Raymond. *Keywords: a vocabulary of culture and society*. São Paulo: Boitempo, 2007.

of common interests, that is, common sense, popular and government by the people.

Unlike *default* standards and issues relating to actions, even in the dimension of ideals, the concepts with the most diverse meanings are "democracy" and "innovation". And, in contemporary practice, there are still realizations and interpretations that express the most indeterminate meanings for these terms. Especially "innovation", which has begun to be understood as an illusion, the abstraction of a future. Especially in Brazil, the city of São Paulo, which represents to the world the image of one of the global metropolises and is seen as a powerhouse for the "possibilities of innovation". [54]In contrast, São Paulo's presence is not like that of Paris or even Berlin. Far away and close at the same time. Far away in time, due to the lack of cultural formation in the German sense of *Bildung* and the French sense of *culture*, but close when time makes all knowledge available to the people, as long as they can have it. In reality, according to research[55] , we see a social inequality in education, which the majority of society does not have. It is therefore a privileged minority that has the opportunity to take an interest in knowledge. This reality, despite appearing to be "uncommon" in German history, not infrequently shows that the difference exists, and can only be seen in statistics and for reasons outside of one's control. There is also a significant situation with the French.

However, it is worth noting that the presence and influence of a Brazilian and global metropolis began not with Western philosophy and a legacy of Franco-German thought, with its origins in Greek antiquity, but as a colony. The philosopher Olgària Matos, a scholar of the German and French schools and a professor at the University of Sao Paulo, presents the essay *Brasil: a memória em trompe-l'œil [Brazil: memory in trompe-l'œil],* through which we can understand why Brazilians and citizens of the world believe in the illusion of Brazil as a "country of the future"[56] . In the words of

---

54 Cf. WAGNER, Christiane. *Aesthetics: contemporary image.* 2013. Thesis - Faculty of Architecture and Urbanism, University of São Paulo, São Paulo, 2013. p. 93. [...] One country we can cite as an example of a creative and economic model for contemporary aesthetic fashion is France. [...].

55 Brazilian Institute of Geography and Statistics (IBGE). *Synthesis of Social Indicators - An analysis of the living conditions of the Brazilian population 2012*
Available at:<http://www.ibge.gov.br/home/estatistica/pesquisas/pesquisas.php> Accessed on: 08/06/2012.

56 "Brazil, country of the future" was originally the title of an essay by Austrian writer Stefan Zweig. A refugee from the Second World War, he arrived in Brazil in 1940 and was dazzled by the landscape and the rhythm of life in Rio de Janeiro.

the philosopher:

"Brazil, it has already been said, does not have a colonial unconscious, inscriptions of a collective history that would show who we are today. From this perspective, [...] it would be difficult to build democracy, because we would lack a representable memory, that is, a contestable one. [...] Vertigo of space and time, Brazil is marked more by the imaginary than by the real. It's a *trompe-l'œil* culture, an optical illusion that leads to destabilization and 'delirium' and, consequently, to the ambivalence of all the senses, so that we come to see unreality as reality."[57]

Matos presents the Brazilian reality in relation to illusion. Referring to Freud's work on illusion, the philosopher presents the Brazilian people as seeking satisfaction, happiness in their life experiences, by possessing something, contemplating and hoping. However, her analysis follows the characteristics of the supposed image Brazilians have of themselves, the lack of historical memory. However, this forgetfulness is possibly attributed to historical events that take place without any ruptures being recorded. Unlike Western Europe, where the French Revolution was a major historical breakthrough. It was the milestone in the conquest of a presence in the public sphere based on legislation and moral values, transforming political and social behavior in Western Europe. However, in Brazil, the process of the relationship between the private and public spheres followed more liberal ideals than social ones, according to our understanding of what Matos writes about Brazilian democracy. It is thus understood that Brazilian democracy has its characteristics in the very relationship of a history of non-identification with the past legacy of colony. Therefore, by continuing history and ignoring its origins as a colony, Brazil followed the linearity of time without memory. The philosopher's words clarify the matter:

"[...] our tradition is one of non-interruption or evanescent memory. From Brazil as a colony to Independence, from the Empire to the Republic, from slavery to abolition, from dictatorships to democracy, there was no temporal interruption, but a continuity through the 'interdiction of the past' - which appears in an exemplary way in the 'transition' or the process of 'opening up' towards the end

Later, however, this expression was used politically by the government of Getúlio Vargas, with the aim of giving hope to Brazilian society that the future of the country would be in his administration." Waldenyr Caldas, during an interview.

57 MATOS, Olgària. *Contemporaneities. Essay, Brazil: memory in trompe-l'œil.* Sào Paulo: Companhia Editora Nacional, 2009, p. 13.

of the period of declared authoritarianism in more recent history."[58]

The year 1985 saw the beginning of the democratic process in Brazil. The dictatorship came to an end with the government of the last military president, Joâo Figueiredo. However, a year earlier, in 1984, the national civil movement *Diretas Jà* began, demanding direct presidential elections in Brazil. Its main leader was Tancredo Neves, who was elected president in 1985 by the Electoral College, but died shortly afterwards. However, the hope of a future for the new generation remained, expressed in Milton Nascimento's song, *Coraçào de Estudante.*

"I want to talk about something Guess where she is? it must be inside our chests or walking through the air it could be right next door much closer than we think the leaf of youth is the right name for this love its moments have been pruned its destiny has been diverted its boyish smile how many times has it been hidden but hope is renewed new dawn, every day and we have to take care of the sprout so that life can give us flowers and fruit a student's heart we have to take care of life we have to take care of the world take care of friendship joy and a lot of dreams scattered along the way green: plant and feeling leaves, heart, youth and faith"[59]

In 1985, with the inauguration of José Sarney, the 1988 Constitution[60] was promulgated, establishing a democratic state of law and a presidential republic. In 1989, Brazil went through the troubled presidency of Fernando Collor de Mello, followed by his removal and succession by his vice-president Itamar Franco. 1989 was a year that marked many changes, not only in Brazil, but throughout the world. The Technological Revolution and the consequences of open borders for globalization, as we discussed in *Urban Reconfigurations, "Polis-ideology"*[61] . We discussed the ideal of democracy in the world and its aspects of realization from that moment on, and the long road to equalizing differences, with reference to equal rights, but in practice, consolidation was a long way off.

Today, when we talk about the mandates of President Fernando Henrique Cardoso, elected in 1994 and re-elected in 1998, we necessarily associate them with the transformations that have taken place in our economy. From the information provided

58. *Ibid.,* p. 16.

59 . Lyrics *from Coraçâo de estudante*, by Wagner Tiso and Milton Nascimento Source: <http://www.miltonnascimento.com.br>. Accessed on: 29/05/2012

60 BRAZIL. *Constitution (1988).* Constitution of the Federative Republic of Brazil. Brasilia, DF: Senado, 1988.

61 WAGNER, Christiane. *Aesthetics: contemporary image. 2013.* Thesis, Faculty of Architecture and Urbanism, University of São Paulo, São Paulo, 2013.

by sociologist Waldenyr Caldas, we can place ourselves in the context from the beginning of his first term, when the country went through a difficult economic and social situation due to uncontrolled inflation. Society lacked a stable economy. One of the consequences was unemployment. Therefore, without being able to plan the economy, purchasing power and the conditions for balancing the market and society were lacking. During this period, Brazilian society experienced a new economic plan created by the Fernando Henrique Cardoso government - the *Real Plan*. Calda says:

"It was created on solid foundations and very different from previous plans. After a long time, the Brazilian economy did indeed recover, and it continues to do so to this day. Since then, the distribution of the wealth produced by the country has improved considerably. Segments of the more modest social classes began to have greater purchasing power, the circulation of wealth increased and it became possible to have a planned economy as we see today. Internationally, the Fernando Henrique government established a very intelligent policy. Since then, Brazil has taken leading positions in some international issues."[62]

In the international context, however, Brazil's reality needs to be understood and this requires space for opinions to be expressed. But we don't need to discuss this in our study. However, it is worth noting that from 1994 to 2002, Brazil did indeed experience national and international recovery. Since then, President Lula, Fernando Henrique Cardoso's successor, has sensibly pursued the *Real Plan* throughout his eight years in office, seeking to stabilize the country's economy. Since 1989, these national transformations and the new image that has emerged in the world have been influenced by digital technology and technological convergence. This great influence on global communication has enabled the *media* to acquire the power they have today. In addition, all globalization has its origins in the Anglo-Saxon ideals of a liberal market economy, which the hegemony of the United States in the 1990s and the entire industry confirmed. This economic power made it possible to invest heavily in the development of information technology. However, it's worth remembering that a new generation is participating very intensely in this new conquest of public space through the Internet.

---

62 Waldenyr Caldas observes that common sense has prevailed over the different political party orientations between the PSDB (Brazilian Social Democratic Party) and the PT (Workers' Party) when it comes to managing the country's economy. The best proof of this is the country's noticeable improvement. Information provided by the sociologist for this study [personal message]. Message received in May 2012.

This new generation has experienced a period of rapid change. But in some cultures, this generation still retains the values of a tradition, such as European culture. In others, especially in Brazil, they no longer have ties to a past. Even more so when there is no tradition and, therefore, "no memory" of its origins, the presence of a global metropolis, under the influence of the American hegemonic force, continues to be marked. With the exception, of course, of a generation of European immigrants[63] who still maintain their roots in the European tradition. As well as the Japanese tradition.

But in the broad sense, there is no shortage of examples of an immigrant culture[64] that has taken over Brazil. All we have to do is look at and remember our cultural environment, starting with the top-grossing films, and remembering the influence of American culture[65] through the *shopping malls* and, of course, credit! It is these examples, among many others, that leave us in no doubt as to what Olgaria Matos wrote in her essay, that democracy in Brazil is relative to its very existence, with the lack of memory of a past that marked it negatively. This shows a "carnivalized sublimation[66] " - the author reuses a term used by Dostoevsky - "pleasure and freedom more than asceticism and virtue, a right in the city, a duty of the state".[67] Without a past, to better understand this idea of "parents of the future". The international image that has been built up of a Brazil Through the observations of the essay cited in the book *Contemporaneidades*, the author directs us towards a "truth" of Brazilian society that is related to the permanence of violence and injustice as the reality of the national image. It is thus identified that this Brazilian reality is really due to the fact, to time in its continuity. History has followed and, with the lack of ruptures and marks, the people

63 Brazilian Institute of Geography and Statistics (IBGE). *The German contribution to the formation of Brazilian culture.* Available at: < http://www.ibge.gov.br/brasil500/alemaes/contribuicao.html>.
Accessed on: 20/05/2012.

64 "On a daily basis, we meet representatives of different peoples from all over the world, and their descendants, who one day arrived in Brazil, bringing their customs, beliefs and ideas. Italians, Poles, Russians, Portuguese, Arabs, Africans, Japanese." Brazilian Institute of Geography and Statistics (IBGE). *Brazil and its immigrants.* Available at: <http://www.ibge.gov.br/ibgeteen/datas/imigrante/brasil e os imigrantes.html>.
Accessed on: 30/05/2012.

65 "Figures from 1936 already show the overwhelming presence of American cinema. 65% of the films shown came from the USA, while national productions were second in the market (26%). At the beginning of the 1950s and 1960s, national films came to represent 32% of the total distributed."
Brazilian Institute of Geography and Statistics (IBGE). *Statistics of the 20th century.* Available at:
<http://www.ibge.gov.br/home/presidencia/noticias/29092003estatisticasecxxhtml.shtm>. Accessed on: 03/06/2012.

66 *Ibid.*, p.13

67 *Ibid.*, p. 19

cannot pay attention to the important events. In this way, without experiences of ruptures, people cannot learn and build the new. There is a sense of "fabulous" and multicultural history that the lack of a cultural heritage turns into an illusion, in other words, the daily *trompe-l'œil*. Since, in the Freudian sense, only something that has already been perceived can become conscious. And therefore, anything other than a feeling, in order to become conscious, would depend on a representation by means of a reference for its materialization. Ideas in the unconscious only become conscious through a link in the preconscious state, in reference to some experience. Not feelings. They are unconscious or conscious, they don't follow any reference, any link and they are contrary to a reason. Because without being able to organize them, without having a parameter to guide them, they can't even find a rational meaning. We've noticed that many people give a pejorative meaning to the term rational, by interpreting it as a lack of feeling, using the expression "coldness".

Which is not true, because it would be a "feeling of coldness". Therefore, the ability to organize, select, compare, value and have discernment is only possible through knowledge and experience - the relationship between reason and sensitivity - so as to be able to evaluate with conscious ideas and expose any feeling, even the "coldest" ones. Rationality thus tries not to delude itself and to balance itself out. But for Brazil, from the point of view of the philosopher Olgaria Matos, we understand it as a country that lacks its memories, its memory and that, as a result, this fact leads it to illusion, due to the lack of a reference of links with history. In this way, we understand that, in the words of the philosopher:

"[...] the positive attributes of illusion, often underestimated: they would be 'delightful', 'that would make happiness come true'. So much so that to 'lose' illusions is to succeed enchantment with disenchantment, to look coldly at what once seduced, is to become disillusioned. The opposite of disillusionment is illusion - 'the joy or happiness one experiences from the possession, contemplation or hope of something'."[68]

The artistic and cultural achievements characterized as Brazilian social reality on a

---

68 MATOS, Olgària. *Contemporaneities. Essay, Brazil: memory in trompe-l'oeil.* Sao Paulo: Companhia Editora Nacional, 2009, p. 14.

national level are telenovelas and carnival. But the great international presence of Brazilian artistic production, apart from a few names in architecture, visual arts and cinema, is in Brazilian popular music. Waldenyr Caldas's *A cultura politico-musical brasileira*[69] provides an insight into Brazil's political history through its popular music. With popular song, Brazilian reality becomes a narrative of its socio-political history. From colonial Brazil to the present day, the rhythm and sound of its origins have recorded both the good and the bad moments of Brazilian reality. The musical repertoire is so vast, with such a strong representation of this culture - well marked throughout the world - that even the most inattentive wouldn't miss hearing many of these records of Brazil's history at some point, whether in the country or around the world. With expressions of an African origin, the lundu and the maxixe stand out in the formation of Brazilian popular song, not only because of their importance at the end of slavery, but from the moment that Europeans also approached this rhythm - the lundu. In this way, the aesthetic transformation gave rise to the Afro-Brazilian rhythm, without changing the formal characteristics, keeping the instruments and the rhythm. The most important thing to know is that the lundu was another instrument in the struggle for black liberation, for aesthetic and behavioral transformation in relation to European culture. Another very significant aspect for the expression of Brazilian popular song was the time the country lived under authoritarian and repressive power. This was a real experience: "songs with a political content were only broadcast on the radio when they praised the Estado Novo", and there was no room for illusions: "some that challenged the Estado Novo were destroyed, and their authors imprisoned[70] ".

However, in the music of exaltation, the figure of Getúlio Vargas in the Estado Novo was praised. A large number of samba-exaltation compositions are part of this repertoire, with the first appearance of the image of "Brazil, *my Brazilian Brazil*" in the composition *Aquarela do Brasil*, by Ary Barroso.

Brazilian culture, freed from authoritarianism in 1945, began to experience the period of developmentalist politics in the early 1950s, with international prominence under

---

69 CALDAS, W. *A Cultura Politico-Musical Brasileira.* São Paulo: Musa Editora, 2005.
70 *Ibid.*, p. 26.

the government of President Juscelino Kubitschek. The country's international image was present not only with the construction of Brasilia, by Lucio Costa and Oscar Niemeyer, as initially presented, but also with bossa nova - initially extolling the beauty of the country and, at the beginning of the 1960s, becoming politicized - this rhythm was a new way of interpreting samba and relied on the resources of the television image and the mass media in the urban environment and across borders. To this day, this rhythm is Brazil's image in many countries, an image shaped by composers Antônio Carlos Jobim and Vinicius de Moraes: *Garota de Ipanema,* the most played Brazilian song in the world.

Little time has passed and from 1964 to 1985 Brazil experienced yet another period of authoritarian state control. And Brazilian popular music, with its strength greater than other artistic manifestations, played a major role in the fight for freedom of expression. Finally, since 1985 and with the 1988 constitution, since 1989, with the borders open to the world and with hopes in the ideals of democracy, plus the re-establishment of the economy under the Fernando Henrique government, the Brazilian people have come to believe in Brazil again. Much more oriented by the hope of a new possibility, of change and at a pace of "where is the world going?" alluding to Edgar Morin's work, *Where is the world going?*[71] to think about the image of the international context. However, Brazil is marked by immigration and hospitality[72] , as Olgaria Matos rightly observes when she quotes Chico Buarque's song, *A Cançào Paratodos*, exemplifying the strong expression of a people who are closer to a community due to the characteristics of a land of origin common to all, with opportunities and optimism for living together in the same space "for all".

We understand this meaning together with the fact that in a community, the values of affection are present in politics as an experience of life in common, unlike a society in which, before the individual can be understood as a human being, they need to be a citizen, following legislation and customs before their human qualities are recognized.

71 MORIN, Edgar. *Where is the world going?* Paris : Éditions de L'Herne, 2007.
72 The origins of this Brazilian hospitality are explained in the following book: HOLLANDA, Sérgio Buarque de. *Roots of Brazil.* Rio de Janeiro: José Olimpo Editora, 1979.

Unlike what happened in previous years under President Fernando Henrique Cardoso and Luiz Inácio Lula da Silva, our country's political situation has undergone structural changes. Until then, we had been experiencing economic stability with an improvement in society's standard of living, with the social mobility of the lower classes, an increase in consumption and greater participation by the population in cultural events, especially in the arts. It could even be said that this mobility has brought great stimulus to the arts and other segments of entertainment culture. After all, the country's economy was developing well and, as a result, politics was cohesive. The three branches of government were balanced and democracy was strengthened. Unfortunately, this framework for the Brazilian state has not remained stable, precisely because of disagreements between the executive and legislative branches. A power struggle that is extremely damaging to society. As a result, Brazilian society is experiencing a moment of economic, political and social destabilization. This is the beginning of a serious crisis of trust in society and in the government itself. Towards the end of President Lula's second term in office, allegations of political corruption took over the country's media. Since then, we have found ourselves in a deep moral crisis, which is reflected in the economy and politics of society and in the National Congress itself. What's more, all sectors of production have been affected, including the cultural industry. Inflation has inhibited people's purchasing power. The consumption of cultural products, including artistic production, has been severely affected by this situation. The arts and investments in the country's ecological balance have shrunk and show no signs of recovery. All investment in the preservation of the Amazon and ecological policies has been suspended in the face of the economic crisis.

Brazil is going through a delicate political moment and, at the same time, is trying to recover by fighting corruption with rare competence. Unlike in previous situations, this time Brazilian society has decided to organize itself and react to the corrupt. Historically, this has never happened before. This is undoubtedly the result of the re-democratization of the country since 1985, when the military was removed from power.

In general, Brazil's cultural and artistic heritage has an international presence in popular music, but it also has great prestige in literature, with Guimaraes Rosa, Machado de Assis and Jorge Amado standing out. In poetry, Carlos Drummond de Andrade. In the visual arts, Lasar Segall, Cândido Portinari, Antônio Dias, Hélio Oiticica, Ligia Clark, Franz Krajcberg, Siron Franco and Claudio Tozzi stand out. In cinema, Glauber Rocha and Walter Salles.

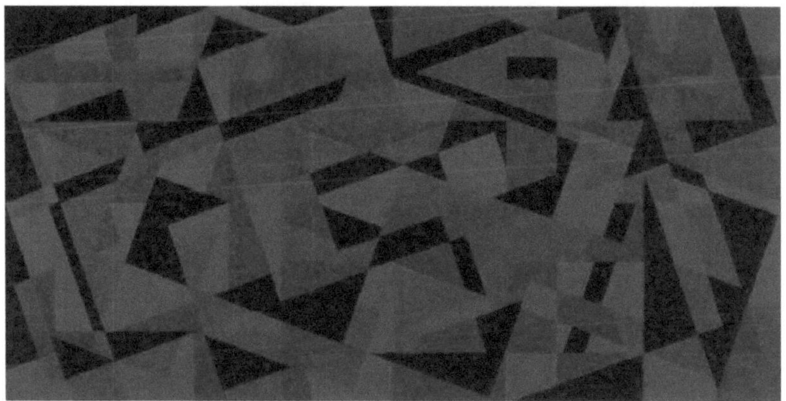

Claudio Tozzi, *Territory*, 2016

The image of a global metropolis began to be built up from the 1990s onwards, whether this was the image of Brazil, with its re-democratization, or that of Germany, with reunification and also re-democratization since it was united, or France during the period of François Mitterrand, and above all, a European Community that gradually built up a common market. A community that was economically consolidated in 1999 with a single currency, the euro. This symbol of a commercial and economic power came into circulation in 2002 and thus marked a new phase of globalization at the turn of the 20th century into the 21st. In the context of creativity, the biggest challenge has been the market, new technologies, production and sales strategies. The world of art was no exception. It's the logic of the market. However, it has become more favorable to the production and consumption of images, as long as profit is made. But, of course, those who "always win are the capitalists[73] , as we learned in Karl Marx's lessons on

73 PETERS, Jorg; ROLF, Bernd. *Was ist ein gerechter Lohn?* Karl Marx. Texte und Materialien für den Unterricht. Kant & Co. Im Interview. Fiktive Gesprache mit Philosophen über ihre Theorien. Stuttgart: Reclam, 2009.

surplus value. In fact, his theories have become even more evident to Marxists, because today, what is most excluded in the *world trade center* are reflections on surplus *value,* so the need to exclude it has made it - by its absence - the most noticeable, and its presence would provoke reflections contrary to the objectives of profit for profit, developed by *marketing.* Let's also remember the power that images have acquired through the new communication technologies and the dimension that social networks and access to the *World Wide Web have* given to globalization. So much so that the Brazilian Micro and Small Business Support Service (Serviço Brasileiro de Apoio às Micro e Pequenas Empresas - SEBRAE) carried out a survey [74] , which began in June 2001 and ended in February 2002, to identify the *Brazilian Face,* the title of the publication of this survey's report, with the aim of characterizing an image that "we didn't have before", or rather, that we want to build for Brazil - the image of business - by means of a survey with the objectives of market strategy and communication with all the techniques of persuasion in building a positive image. Including a predominance of the term "innovation". But the meaning of innovation in the business world has become, like any commodity, worn out and obsolete.

If you resist, it's just a term to stimulate the appearance of something that might have value. Above all, it's a *marketing* technique, feeding consumer desires and expectations. Even Anglo-Saxon universities are following the logic of productivity in search of innovation, with international *rankings.* And they are demanding innovation from their researchers through their regulations. What result is expected? That all researchers can innovate? If this is possible, as, for example, happened with Copernicus and Kepler, then we would need other worlds or a long time to be recognized. Because a single world wouldn't be able to support so much innovation. And as far as time is concerned, humanity would need to be above the supposed geniuses or super-entrepreneurs of innovation in order to accept the supposed innovations as immediately as they were found. But the business world itself is finally realizing that it needs to

74 SEBRAE, Brazilian Micro and Small Business Support Service. *Cara Brasileira: Brazilianness in business - a path to "made in Brazil".*
Brasilia-DF: SEBRAE Nacional, 2002.

innovate[75] its strategies to stimulate production, without the wear and tear of this term causing even more pointless competition, which, as always, has its winners - because they have an advantage over others thanks to some actions that may or may not be surpassed. In order to do this, we want the best and therefore depend on many things that go beyond the dimension of experience. In this sense, knowledge through experience keeps us in history, and as Edgar Morin observes, countries in the process of development are beginning again the histories of European socialism and the history of apparatus socialism (*socialisme d'appareil*), and these histories even return and coexist in a progressive or even regressive way. Let's consider the advances and returns in their constant repetition, as mentioned above, referring to the vicissitudes of life. Thus, it is in this sense that Morin expresses the need to pay attention to the planetary emergence of humanity or the emergence of planetary humanity. Of course, nothing is off the planet as far as the history of civilization is concerned. Today's experiences include those of the past. But it is not yet a characteristic that can be attributed to the planet as a whole, nor even its end. Morin reminds us:

"Fifty thousand years ago, homo sapiens emerged on all continents, and the human diaspora has been consolidated for thousands of years. Ethnic groups are infirmed in their language, their culture and their beliefs. Civilizations communicated from beginning to end, but the great dérive had isolated the humanities of America, Africa, Asia and Europe from each other, and within the vast continents, empires and civilizations remained ignorant of each other. Il y avait des histoires, variées, multiples, asynchrones, non pas une histoire."[76]

Now, in the 21st century, humanity presents itself in its cultural diversity as a planetary reality under the tutelage of technology and communication. But even through this ease and proximity, and even in a single reality, humanity is still diverse. In its continuity,

---

75 The São Paulo newspaper Valor Econômico has an article on the term "innovation" published on May 25, 26 and 27, 2012, in the Technology & Communications section, translating an article from the American newspaper, The Wall Street Journal, by journalist Leslie Kwoh, in which she discusses the fact that the term "innovation" is becoming a cliché in the business dictionary. The article begins with the following sentence: "Does your company innovate? Almost all of them would say yes."

76 "Fifty thousand years ago, *homo sapiens* spread across all continents, and the human diaspora continued, consolidated, for millennia. Ethnicities were closed in on their language, their culture and their beliefs. Civilizations progressively communicated and came closer together, but the great deviation was that they were isolated from each other, the humanities of America, Africa, Asia, Europe and, even within the vast continents, empires and civilizations remained ignorant of each other. There were histories, asynchronous varieties, multiple or many, but not a single history." (MORIN, Edgar. *Where is the world going?* Paris: L'Herne, 2007. p. 54-55.

however, with the need for an illusion for creations, which so many other artistic achievements have madc possible. Believing that illusion is important is a subject of divided opinion, but we don't know from experience how important it is not to have it. We think only of Plato's ideas, removing artists from the republic. But in reality, artists always form a reality. Even if their art can offer an illusion. Even so, in the current planetary crisis, Morin says that even though many people may believe that if they lose their illusions, they would lose everything, this is a mistake. For this thinker, we would make a prodigious achievement by losing our mistakes, that is, the conscience needed to decide the future. Thus, in the Cartesian sense, we understand this consciousness in the game (*ludere*) of mistakes and successes, that is, in its sense, by the illusion (also *ludere*) as a game in its *default* parameters, of the possibilities of mistakes and successes, of errors and, finally, of illusions by illusions. However, Morin deals with the loss that humanity has experienced with the promise of progress, and which was at the same time great progress, discovering that progress is a myth. What we see is a value system that operates through instability and insecurity, and seeks security by establishing optimistic prognoses. We can see this dynamic in industry and commerce, in universities, in the arts and in politics, as we have well exemplified throughout this analysis. But this whole relationship with the image of success and the search for innovation is the reason for communication and its reality. So, faced with the paradoxes of the *media* relationship verified by studies[77] , on the one hand, it is possible for the individual to choose, to select information and, on the other, that the power of the *media* consists in its ability to construct a reality.

The *media,* social networks, everything is converging on a recent major event, which is a great reality in the global metropolises, and which, due to so much other news and illusory images, few people do not realize the reality of what is being announced, perhaps those who are not aware of technological convergence or who have no sense of history. For example, let's remember the indignados movement. A necessary movement in the face of so many inequalities and injustices that originated *in* Stéphane

77 Cf. Interview with Prof. Dr. Waldenyr Caldas.

Hessel's work, Be Outraged, with the intention of warning humanity. Stéphane Hessel, a naturalized French resistance fighter born in Berlin in 1917, had a history [78] of many experiences and took part in the committee responsible for drawing up what would become the Universal Declaration of Human Rights.

In this book, *Indigne* vos, the author tells the complex world of today about the reality in which humanity finds itself, from his own experience and knowledge at the turn of the 20th century, having participated in the main events that revolutionized the world in the 20th century and, above all, in the search for human rights, calling for a networked struggle and joint action, in which indignation is necessary, and affirms to everyone who will build the 21st century, in his book *Indigne vos!* with one last phrase: "To create is to resist. To resist is to create."

---

78 Stéphane Hessel, in his long life, had a succession of reasons to be indignant. He was marked by Sartre, an older disciple, who taught him that the individual's responsibility does not lie in trusting in a power or a god. It is therefore necessary to engage in the name of responsibility as a human person. He was a disciple of Hegel and a student of Merleau-Ponty. But his natural tendency to optimism, to believe that desires can be possible, led him to Hegel's theories, to the sense of man's freedom in progress in constant stages. And so, said this gentleman who died on February 27, 2013 at the age of 95: "History is made up of successive shocks, the challenges are taken into account." Marked by many hardships and surviving as a French diplomat, he continued his missions for humanity. But his story had its roots in the arts and literature: his father, Franz Hessel, had a friend who used to visit his home to translate Marcel Proust's *In Search of Lost Time* together. Translated from French into German. This friend was Walter Benjamin. Stéphane Hessel arrived in Paris in 1924 with his father and his mother Helen Grund, also a writer, painter and music lover. At the time, they frequented the Parisian avant-garde. Marcel Duchamp and Alexander Calder were part of their family life. Her parents' story inspired François Truffaut's 1962 film adaptation of Henri-Pierre Roche's novel *Jules et Jim.* Their story is of great importance as a witness to human reality in the 20th and early 21st centuries. Much of the study in my thesis (WAGNER C., 2013) was based on the reality of Stéphane's story, but in another version, of the arts as a witness to humanity, through all possible feelings, at the limit of time, between nations, in order to constitute knowledge through images. Cf.: WAGNER, Christiane. *Aesthetics: contemporary image.* 2013. Faculty of Architecture and Urbanism, University of São Paulo, São Paulo, 2013. HESSEL, Stéphane. *Be indignant!* Translated by Marli Peres. São Paulo: Leya, 2011.
Id. Indignez-vous! Indigène editions, 2011.

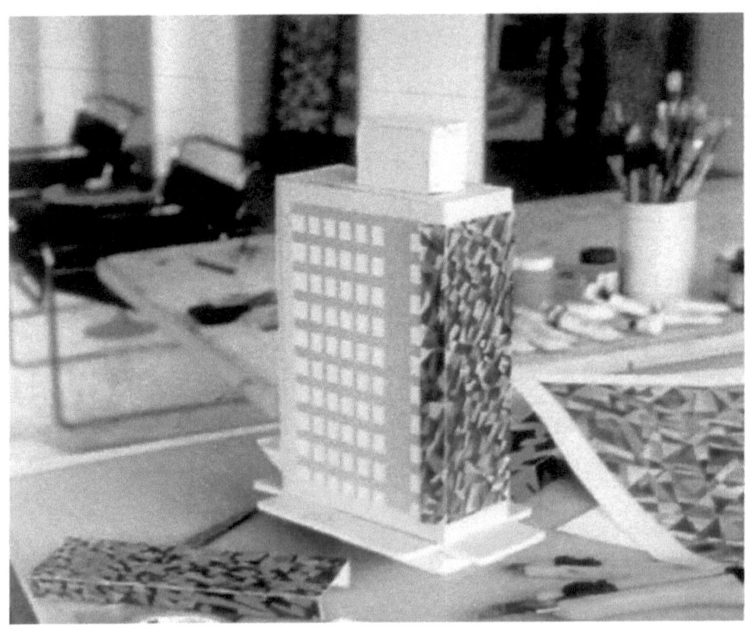

Claudio Tozzi, *Exclusive Building Project*, 2003

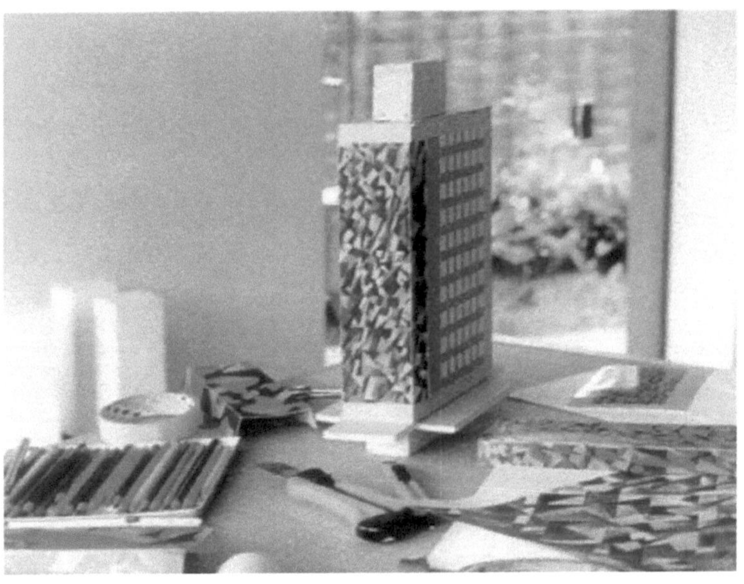

Claudio Tozzi, *Exclusive Building Project*, 2003

Final considerations

It is on the basis of the principles of production and the world scenario that the socio-philosophical analysis of this research into aesthetics is based. This scenario is part of unlimited development, followed by an increase in economic activity, the net value of goods produced and the aim of better quality as a result of innovation. Consequently, it contributes to cultural transformations through new resources and technologies. We discussed the image as an artistic idea and realization, in the public space, in its historical and political context, in order to highlight elements, among many, that are the most significant and that perpetuate on the plane of human existence. Aside from all the value and power relations in societies and cultures, the first thing discussed was technique and the main influences in the West that led to the transformations. The dome element, whose form and function have always been an important element since ancient and primitive civilizations, was presented with great emphasis, mainly because of the symbolic construction it has always represented. Through their form, the idea of the universe has always prevailed, or of encompassing life, or even of an underground world, through ideas, ideologies, doctrines, dogmas and, always prevailing, the desire to materialize power or domination, through the dome, through its most varied forms of construction and predominant techniques, in styles and periods. We can think of the most prestigious architectures in the history of art, but in this study we will limit ourselves to examples of the main domes that symbolize power in contemporary France, Brazil and Germany. Specifically, the domes and their contexts in the history of Brazil, France and Germany, in order to emphasize public space as a dimension of humanity that is oriented towards concreteness. A space that, in the midst of relationships of empirical values, leads us towards the universe of ideas, making us feel the power of the universe, of nature and of ideas that strengthen achievements.

The correspondences around contemporary images follow the models of good manners, well-being, consumer satisfaction, products and services, under the exemplary model of the family, of work, of all the desires that the bourgeois wish to fulfill. Then, as exchange values and use values correspond, we find the effects of cultural transformations, as already mentioned, which constitute the rhythm of a renewal, of a materialized dynamic with only differentiation as the means of innovation. A process through which individuals can ideologize, imagine in the proper sense of the word: create images. At the same time as individuals' need for productive achievements is expected, new forms are expected so that the system can produce its goods. This is the condition of the system itself, to produce "the difference" in order to obtain new demands, in other words, the continuity of production for needs to the extent of social correspondences through the means of signification. The rhythm of social correspondence revolves around the production of capitalist ideology, through the images that translate the essential ideas to ensure the system of consumption. For the majority, images are the product of consumption. Consumption is the main medium in which competition exerts its advertising power, producing images through which the entire urban social universe is attributed, through the acculturation of traditional, rural or marginal communities. All citizens are integrated into this process, which is the rhythm of capitalism's ideological correspondences. There is not a single condition in which the cultural industry can have its own desire without it being in the process of differentiation.

It is the logic of differentiation that accompanies all the analysis of this research into the configuration of the contemporary image, because the economic development of society is characterized by differentiation. The idea of a majority, of a standardization of taste, would refer to the idea of being subject to a democratization of taste. This would be impossible, because it is a subjectivity of the human essence, which is unique to each existence. Moreover, economists have long known that it is growth that is responsible for discrimination.

In addition to the fundamental bibliography, the study of the theories of Jürgen Habermas, one of the last active representatives of the Frankfurt School, was also justified. In his work *The Theory of Communicative Action*[79] , he analyzes two dimensions that coexist in society: the system and the world of life. The system deals

79 HABERMAS, Jürgen. *Kommunikatives Handeln und detranszendentalisierte Vernunft*. Reclam Verlag, Stuttgart, 2001. *Theorie des kommunikativen Handelns*, 1981 (*Théorie de l'agir communicationnel*, 1987).

with material reproduction, the logic of technology in a process of adaptation according to objectives, maintaining political-social, cultural and economic relations. For the lifeworld dimension, he discusses symbolic reproduction, language, by analyzing the compositions of networks of meanings referring to objective facts, social norms or subjective contents. Expressivity is the representation of experience, according to Habermas' analysis of the individual's own subjective world and its correspondence with society, in the name of truth, which can be acquired through privileged access to an experience with the outside world. Expressions are also rational and all imaginations are represented, i.e. in Althusser's sense, ideologization can be accepted by the community as long as it is comprehensible. This ideologization is in a state of evaluation and in the name of the same reasons that consumer society is guided by, in the face of value judgments. Starting from rational communication through phenomenological analysis, Habermas developed a concept of the rational practice of communication, which means the resolution, the discursive evaluation of each intended expression (*Geltungsansprüche*). Discourse or argumentation is decisive in the instance of rational behavior. Habermas distinguishes between theoretical discourse, practical discourse, aesthetic criticism, therapeutic criticism and the explanatory discourses that the *media* reflect so that the goal of communication - which rests on a reason that consists of improving discourse - can be made accessible and relevant through learning procedures.

The work of Jürgen Habermas and Edgar Morin was taken as the theoretical axis for this reflection. These thinkers have acquired a great deal of knowledge about the transition from the 20th to the 21st century. They have contributed to a view of the world from a new perspective, where the individual is capable of creating new realities, determining the emergence of new forms of representation of their ideals through technology and the convergence of the media, hypermedia and the *media* as objects of new theories in aesthetics and, above all, to help conceptualize the status of the contemporary image and the daily life of a metropolis.

Theories of perception are hypotheses. In certain situations, they are confirmed, disregarded or modified. In general, in perception, an individual's actions have been established for a long time by perceptual activity acquired before the start of a new action in a given situation. The individual chooses, organizes and transforms the information they receive from the environment.

These pieces of information are indications or signs that serve to evoke the hypothesis, to confirm it or not. Perception is an interpretation, it doesn't imply any guarantee of validity or certainty, it remains in the realm of the probable. In this way, as with any probable knowledge, in order to be validated, perception needs to be subjected to proof, to be confirmed or not. It is understood that the configuration of the image consists of the problematics of perception. At the same time, this is the process through which facts are translated into knowledge for the realization, configuration and formation of images, based mainly on the relationships between mental images and external reality, exposing itself to the probability of illusion.

The clearest dimension of the presence and participation of new visual or artistic projects in contemporary society begins with social, economic and cultural changes and technological transformations that intervene in a conception of the world with its own characteristics and needs, but which can vary according to culture, society and economy. The state creates social policies and proposals for society. These are essential nowadays as stages in an individual's life and as a process that is part of social reality. In this way, contemporary creativity and aesthetics seek innovation in the aspects of the individual's interaction with "social reality". Thus, the main hypothesis of a realistic perfection of the image, with no room for an aesthetic illusion, would be variable because the illusion would not depend specifically on the perfection of an image. It is conditional on the existence of a reality of the image with the aim of illusion. Therefore, it would be possible to imagine reality according to an interpretation based on abstraction, or the processes of creation, as each image presented a new circumstance. This, configured to contemporary standards of aesthetics, with pragmatic objectives in messages transmitted, suggesting innovation. These messages would also be responsible for linking the elements of a symbolic association to the collective imagination. For this reason, we conclude the importance of the secondary hypothesis, of an illusion through the collective imagination capable of recognizing new paradigms in order to discern illusion from reality. Consequently, looking for everyday urban habits in the midst of configuring images that represent reality. Thus, based on the primary and secondary hypotheses, the existence of what would be an innovation for social reality was conditioned by a problematization in the sense of clarifying the influence of cultural production on the configuration of the contemporary image in large metropolises for an urban aesthetic.

Bibliography

ADORNO, Theodor W. *Asthetische Theorie.* Frankfurt: Suhrkamp, 1970.

ARISTOTLE. *Poétique* (transl. J. Hardy). Paris: Gallimard, 1996.

ALTHUSSER, Louis. *On reproduction.* Paris: PUF, 1995.

BAUDRILLARD, Jean. *The system of objects.* Paris: Gallimard, 1968.

. *The consumer society: its myths and structures.*

Paris: Denoël, 1970.

. *Simulacres et Simulation.* Paris: Galilée, 1981.

. *Pour une critique de l'economie politique du signe.*

Paris: Gallimard, 1972.

. *Illusion, désillusion esthétiques.* Paris: Sens & Tonka, 1997.

BENJAMIN, Walter. *Œuvres,* Tome I, II et III. Paris: Gallimard, 2000

BOBBIO, Norberto. *The future of democracy.* Paris: Seuil, 2007.

CALDAS, Waldenyr. *Utopia of taste.* Sao Paulo: Brasiliense, 2009.

. *The culture of youth.* Sao Paulo: Musa, 2008.

. *Brazilian Political-Musical Culture.* Sao Paulo: Musa, 2005.

. *Themes of mass culture: music, soccer, consumption.*

Sao Paulo: Arte e Ciência, 2000.

HABERMAS, Jürgen. *Technik und Wissenschaft als "Ideologie".*

Frankfurt: Suhrkamp, 1968.

. *Kultur undKritik. Verstreute Aufsătze.* Frankfurt: Suhrkamp, 1973.

. *Kommunikatives Handeln und detranszendentalisierte Vernunft.*

Stuttgart: Reclam, 2001.

. *Politik, Kunst, Religion.* Stuttgart: Reclam Verlag, 1978.

. *L'espace publique*. Translated by Marc B. de Launay.

Éditions Payot et Rivages, 1997.

. *Idéalisations et communication - Agir communicatonnel et usage de la raison.* France: Fayard, 2006.

HESSEL, Stéphane. *Be indignant!* Sao Paulo: Leya, 2011.

HOLLANDA, S. Buarque de. *Roots of Brazil.* Rio de Janeiro:

José Olimpo Editora, 1979.

JIMENEZ, Marc. *Qu'est-ce que l'esthétique ?*

Paris: Gallimard, Folio Essais, 1997.

. *L'esthétique contemporaine.* Paris: Klincksieck, 2004.

. *La querelle de l'art contemporain.*

Paris: Gallimard, Folio Essais, 2005.

KANT, Immanuel. *Kritik der reinen Vernunft.*

Stuttgart: Reclam Verlag, 2006.

. *Kritik der praktischen Vernunft.* Stuttgart: Reclam Verlag, 2008.

. *Kant, Le jugement esthétique, textes choisis.* PUF, 2006

LALANDE, André. *Vocabulaire technique et critique de la philosophie.* Paris: Presses Universitaire de France, 2010.

MATOS, Olgària. *Contemporaneities. Essay, Brazil: memory in trompe-l'oeil.* Sao Paulo: Companhia Editora Nacional, 2009

MORIN, Edgar. *Where is the world going?* Paris: Éditions de L'Herne, 2007.

. *Pour entrer dans le siècle XXI.* Paris: Seuil, 2004.

. *The road. Pour l'avenir de l'humanité.* Paris: Fayard, 2011.

SOURIAU, Étienne. *Vocabulaire d'esthétique*. Paris: PUF, 1990.

WILLIAMS, Raymond. *Keywords: a vocabulary of culture and society.* Sao Paulo:

Boitempo Editorial, 2007.

WAGNER, Christiane. *In Art - invention and artifice*. Sao Paulo: Blucher, 2009.

. *Esthétique: l'image contemporaine et l'analyse du concept de l'innovation.* Saarbrücken: Paf, 2014.

. *Aesthetic Experience: Visual Culture as the Masterpiece of Nonhumanity.* On_Culture: The Open Journal for the Study of Culture 2, Giessen, 2016.

http://geb.uni-giessen.de/geb/volltexte/2016/12358/

. *Poïésis : entre la raison et la sensibilité Les nouveaux médiums de l'art.* French Journal for Media Research [online], Full texts, Theatricalization of the Contemporary Politics, 7/2017.

http://frenchjournalformediaresearch.com/lodel/index.php?id=1072

. *Kunstwerke der Neuen Welt: Zeitgenossische brasilianische Kunst*. Munich: GRIN Verlag, 2016

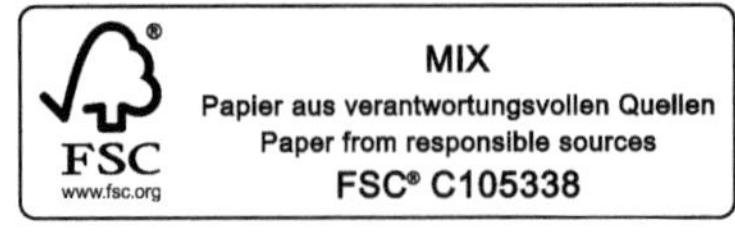

Printed by Books on Demand GmbH, Norderstedt / Germany